LAWRENCE DURRELL

An Illustrated Checklist

Alan G. Thomas

James A. Brigham

Southern Illinois University Press

Carbondale and Edwardsville

Library of Congress Cataloging in Publication Data

Thomas, Alan G.
    Lawrence Durrell, an illustrated checklist.

    An illustrated expansion and updating of the Durrell
bibliography by Alan G. Thomas originally published in:
Lawrence Durrell: a study / by G.S. Fraser.
    Includes index.
    1. Durrell, Lawrence--Bibliography. I. Brigham,
James A.   II. Title.
Z8250.54.T47   1983   016.828'91209   83-6782
[PR6007.U76]
ISBN 0-8093-1021-X

CONTENTS

LIST OF ILLUSTRATIONS

PREFACE

   Lawrence Durrell: An Illustrated Checklist
is offered to all those who believe with William
Cowper that "Books are not seldom talismans and
spells"--to students and to scholars, to book
collectors and to all those for whom one or
another of Durrell's works has come to have a
personal significance. Appropriately, this
Checklist appears in the year following his
selection as one of twenty "Best of British
Authors."

   The first bibliography of Durrelliana was
provided by Derek Stanford in his *The Freedom of
Poetry* (1947). That was a selected bibliography;
so, too, in its way, was Alan G. Thomas and
Lawrence C. Powell's "Some Uncollected Authors,
XXIII: Lawrence Durrell" (1960), which omitted
Durrell's contributions to periodicals. Anthony
Knerr's "Regarding a Checklist of Lawrence
Durrell," published the following year, while it
added to the Thomas-Powell list using their
numbering system, devoted itself primarily to
publications in periodicals. Since 1960, then,
a growing interest in Durrell as a major literary
figure, coupled with the continuing appreciation
in the value of his books as collectors' items,
has led to the appearance of bibliographies in
different contexts. Bernard Stone's bibliography
in Alfred Perlès's *My Friend Lawrence Durrell*
(1961), Robert A. Potter and Brooke Whiting's

Lawrence Durrell: A Checklist (1961), and Alan
G. Thomas's bibliography for G. S. Fraser's
Lawrence Durrell: A Study (1968) are each the
result of a different kind of interest in
Durrell.

This new checklist follows the bibliography
in Fraser's *Study*, and thus keeps to the numbering
system employed by Thomas and Powell. Although
further items have been added to the early
sections of their lists, we have retained the
original numbering in the interests of continuity
and in an effort to avoid confusion. Durrell's
notes are also from that earlier work. Ideally,
this *Illustrated Checklist* would have reproduced
the dustwrappers of all of Durrell's books.
However, as it was our purpose to make the
volume as accessible as possible, and as so many
illustrations would have entailed a substantial
increase in cost to the buyer, we chose to
illustrate those of his works which seemed to us
to be of greatest significance to students,
scholars and collectors alike. The *terminus a
quem* of the work is June 1981, and thus we have
not included such items as Durrell's "Foreword"
to *Fine Books and Book Collecting*, a *festschrift*
in honor of Alan Thomas's seventieth birthday,
or the *Proceedings* of *On Miracle Ground: The
First National Lawrence Durrell Conference*.

We are indebted to friends and colleagues,
both bibliophiles and scholars for their kind
assistance at various points in the preparation
of this book. For their invaluable additions to
the lists, we especially wish to thank John W,
G. Dudley in England, Dr. Hartmut-Ortwin Feistel
in the Republic of West Germany, and Grove Koger
in the United States. Our thanks also go to
Edmund K. Wong and Michael Berger of Audio-
Visual Services, Okanagan College, for their
advice and technical assistance.

All 8vo. and publisher's cloth, unless otherwise
stated. Lawrence Durrell's comments printed in
italic.

1   *QUAINT FRAGMENT: POEMS WRITTEN BETWEEN
     THE AGES OF SIXTEEN AND NINETEEN.* London:
     The Cecil Press, 1931. Portrait. *"Never
     published. Cecil Jeffries bought a hand
     press and asked me to give him something
     to practise with; poems were easier than
     prose so I gave him an old notebook with
     roughs. Title was his. We took two pulls
     I think before the type was dispersed.
     One copy bound."* [This book *is* extremely
     rare, but Durrell's statement that only
     one copy was bound is an exaggeration.
     Three or four have passed through the
     antiquarian book market in the last few
     years, and one copy, left behind in Corfu,
     was destroyed.]

2   *TEN POEMS.* London: The Caduceus Press,
     1932. Wrappers.

     ---. Edition de Luxe. Limited to twelve
     copies, signed by the author. London: The
     Caduceus Press, 1932. Buckram. [The
     author's and publisher's recollections of
     the number printed differ so widely that
     it seems wiser not to quote them. The

number is quite small, the book did not
sell out, and the residue stock was destroyed in the London blitz. The same
applies to A.4. The device on this book
was designed by Nancy Myers, Durrell's
first wife.]

2a   *BALLADE OF SLOW DECAY*. [Bournemouth,
n.p.], Christmas 1932. [A Christmas card.
Two leaves. A device by Nancy Myers on
p. i.]

3   *BROMO BOMBASTES: A FRAGMENT FROM A LACONIC
DRAMA BY GAFFER PEESLAKE, WHICH SAME BEING
A BRIEF EXTRACT FROM HIS COMPENDIUM OF
LISSON DEVICES*. London: The Caduceus
Press, 1933. Boards. [Limited to 100
copies. A squib satirizing Shaw's *Black
Girl*.]

4   *TRANSITION: POEMS*. London: The Caduceus
Press, 1934. Boards. [See note to A.2.]

5   *MASS FOR THE OLD YEAR*. [Bournemouth,
n.p.], New Year 1935. [A New Year card,
with poem on p. iii. Two leaves on
Japanese vellum, 9 x 6 inches. A device
by Nancy Myers on p. iv; she drew carica-
tures on p. i of some copies. Only two
copies are known to have survived: one
bears a pen-and-ink caricature of Alan G.
Thomas suffering from post-Christmas dys-
pepsia; the other, sent to George Wilkinson, is now in the British Museum.]

6   *PIED PIPER OF LOVERS*. London: Cassell,
1935. [Dust jacket designed by Nancy
Myers. Spine incorrectly lettered: *Pied
Pipers of Lovers*.]

7   *PANIC SPRING: A ROMANCE* by Charles Norden.
London: Faber & Faber, 1937. [The first
of Durrell's books to be published by

Faber, who suggested a pseudonym because
Pied Piper of Lovers had been a failure.]

8   *THE BLACK BOOK: AN AGON*. Paris: The
    Obelisk Press, 1938. Wrappers. [Volume
    I of the *Villa Seurat Series*, edited by
    Henry Miller. An erratum slip was added:
    "ERRATUM owing to a mistake in the pagi-
    nation, pages 114, 117, 115, 116, 118
    should be read in that order." The copies
    hitherto examined did not contain the
    erratum slip, from which we conclude that
    it was not added until a number of copies
    had been despatched.]

    ---. Paris: The Olympia Press, 1959.
    Wrappers. [Second edition, with a new
    preface. Promptly banned in Eire.]

    ---. [U.S. edition advertised by Circle
    Editions, Berkeley, California, on the
    backflap of jacket of *Zero* (see A.13),
    but never issued.]

    ---. New York: E. P. Dutton, 1960.
    [Contains the preface to the Olympia Press
    edition (1959). Introduction by Gerald
    Sykes.]

    ---. *Le Carnet Noir*. Paris: Gallimard,
    1961. Translated by Roger Giroux.

    ---. *Die Schwarze Chronik*. Hamburg:
    Rowholt Verlag, 1962. Translated by
    Herbert Zand.

    ---. London: Faber & Faber, 1973.

    ---. London: Faber & Faber, 1977.
    Paperback.

9   *A PRIVATE COUNTRY*. London: Faber & Faber,
    1943.

10   *"PREMATURE EPITAPHS AND ALL."* Alexandria,
      1944. Typescript, handbound in wrappers.
      [Six copies only produced for friends.]

11   *PROSPERO'S CELL: A GUIDE TO THE LANDSCAPE
      AND MANNERS OF THE ISLAND OF CORCYRA.*
      London: Faber & Faber, 1945. Illustrated.

      ---. [U.S. edition advertised in *Chimera*,
      V: 2 (Winter 1947): "Two works of his,
      The Dark Labyrinth and *Prospero's Cell*,
      have been published recently by Reynal
      & Hitchcock." Both books are listed in
      The Publishers Trade List Annual 1946
      under Reynal & Hitchcock. The firm went
      bankrupt before the author's contracts
      were signed, however, and neither book
      was published.]

      ---. New York: E. P. Dutton, 1960.
      [Issued together with *Reflections on a
      Marine Venus* (see A.21).]

      ---. London: Faber & Faber, 1962. Paper-
      back.

      ---. *L'Ile de Prospero.* Paris: Buchet-
      Chastel, 1962. Translated by Roger
      Giroux.

      ---. *Schwarze Oliven. Korfu - Insel der
      Phäaken.* Hamburg: Rowholt Verlag, 1963.
      Translated by Peter Bermback and Herbert
      Zand.

      ---. Hamburg: Rowholt Verlag, 1968.
      Paperback.

      ---. London: Faber & Faber, 1975.
      [With a preface by the author and a new
      chapter, "Lear's Corfu: An Anthology Drawn
      from the Painter's Letters," which was
      originally published by Corfu Travel in

1965 (see C.14).]

---. London: Faber & Faber, 1978. Paperback. [A new jacket by David Gentleman
appeared on the paperback edition.]

---. New York: Penguin Books, 1978.
[A reprint of the 1960 Dutton edition.]

12   *CITIES, PLAINS AND PEOPLE.* London: Faber
     & Faber, 1946.

13   *ZERO AND ASYLUM IN THE SNOW: TWO EXCUR-
     SIONS INTO REALITY.* Rhodes [privately
     printed], 1946. Wrappers. [Block depic-
     ting ship and fish on cover and title.]

13a *TWO EXCURSIONS INTO REALITY.* Berkeley,
     Calif.: Circle Editions, 1947.

14   *THE PARTHENON: FOR T. S. ELIOT.* Rhodes
     [n.p., 1945 or 1946]. Decorated card
     cover. [4 pp.; 7 7/8 x 6 1/4 inches.
     Durrell's own copy bears the following
     note in his hand: *"Lawrence Durrell, his
     copy. This was set and printed in 25
     copies at the Govt. Press in Rhodes,
     Dodecanese Islands, and issued as a
     Christmas Card to friends. The cover had
     been especially cut by an artist for the
     Governor of Rhodes (Italian)."*]

15   *CEFALU: A NOVEL.* London: Editions Poetry
     London, 1947. [Two bindings, green and
     light brown cloth. Author's and British
     Museum copies both green cloth.]

---. *The Dark Labyrinth.* London: Ace
Books, The Harborough Publishing Company,
1958. [While alterations in this reprint
of *Cefalù* were limited to a few sentences,
there were some significant changes made
in the organization of the novel. In the

first place, there was no "Table of
Contents" in the first edition; secondly,
the original was divided into three
separate sections composed of, in the
order in which they now appear, chapters
one through five, six through twelve, and
thirteen and fourteen. Chapter Five, "The
Medium," was originally called "Fearmax."
The most important change, in our view,
was really an omission: beginning with
this edition, the epigram from *The Phaedo*
which appeared in the first edition has
consistently been omitted. We reproduce
it here in the interests of scholarship:
"'Well, and is there not an opposite of
life as sleep is the opposite of waking?'
'True,' he said. 'And what is it?'
'Death,' he said."]

---. [On U.S. edition, 1946, see A.11.]

---. London: Faber & Faber, 1961.

---. *Cefalû*. Paris: Buchet-Chastel,
1961. Translated by Roger Giroux.

---. New York: E. P. Dutton, 1962.

---. *Das Dunkle Labyrinth*. Hamburg:
Rowholt Verlag, 1962. [In spite of the
note "unabridged edition," which is
mostly reserved for paperback reprints of
original hardcover editions, this
paperback is the only German edition.]

---. London: Faber & Faber, 1964.
Paperback.

---. New York: Penguin Books, 1978.
Paperback.

16   *ON SEEMING TO PRESUME*. London: Faber &
Faber, 1948. [First binding brick red

cloth, second binding light red cloth.]

17   *A LANDMARK GONE*. Los Angeles: Reuben
Pearson, 1949. Wrappers. [8 1/2 x 5 3/8
inches. 125 copies privately printed for
Lawrence Clark Powell. Contains "A Note
on Lawrence Durrell" by Lawrence Clark
Powell. *A Landmark Gone* was first pub-
lished in *Middle East Anthology*, edited by
John Waller and Erik de Mauny (See D.15).]

18   *DEUS LOCI: A POEM*. Ischia: Di Maio Vito,
1950. Wrappers. [6 1/4 x 4 1/4 inches.
200 copies privately printed, signed by
the author. Variant colors of covers red,
buff, green, and gray, with no precedence
of issue.]

19   *SAPPHO: A PLAY IN VERSE*. London: Faber
& Faber, 1950.

    ---. New York: E. P. Dutton [1958].
[Sheets of English edition with undated
cancel title.]

    ---. Hamburg: Rowholt Verlag, 1958.
Translated by Ursula and Oscar Fritz
Schuh. [The text of the German acting
edition, as well as of the trade edition
(see below, 1964) contains a number of
changes suggested by Gustav Gründgens.]

    ---. Paris: Gallimard, 1962. Translated
by Roger Giroux.

    ---. *Drei dramatische Dichtungen: Sappho
--Actis--Ein Irischer Faust*. Hamburg:
Rowholt Verlag, 1964. Translated by
Ursula Schuh, Oscar Fritz Schuh, and
Robert Schnorr. With a Foreword by Oscar
Fritz Schuh. [Only German trade edition
of the three plays.]

---. London: Faber & Faber, 1967.   Paperback.

[Margaret Rawlings took the title role in
a rehearsed reading of this play at the
French Institute, London, in 1952.
Terence Tiller's production, broadcast in
the BBC Third Program on 25 March 1957,
starred Jill Balcon. On 28 August 1961,
Margaret Rawlings played Sappho in the
first stage production in English at the
Royal Lyceum Theatre during the Edinburgh
Festival. Elizabeth Flickenschildt took
the title role in the first German stage
production at the Deutsches Schauspielhaus, Hamburg, 21 November 1959. The
program for that production contains an
article on Durrell by Henry Miller (see
D.27 for photographs of the German production). *"Sappho was cut and mounted
under the advice of Gustaf Gründgens;
Acte went through about four drafts, and
some parts were written in as after-
thoughts while the play was in rehearsal.
An exchange of letters between myself and
Gründgens was published by Rowholt Verlag
as a booklet for the opening night. This
was the most successful of the plays in
terms of number of performances. Remember
it played in a repertory cycle with two
other plays - Shaw's Caesar and Schiller's
Mary Stewart, and the advance bookings
determined whether people wanted it
again or not. It lasted the season out.
Faustus was mounted by Oscar Schu in the
same theatre in its printed version quite
entire. It is well constructed whatever
other demerits it has as a piece. I was
unhappy about the hasty writing in Acte
and revised it completely for English
publication."*

20   *KEY TO MODERN POETRY*. London: Peter
        Nevill, 1952. [Lectures given in Argen-
        tina for the British Council.]

        ---. *A Key to Modern British Poetry*.
        Norman: University of Oklahoma Press,
        1952. [Sheets of the English edition.]

        ---. *Key to Modern Poetry*. Calcutta:
        Rupa & Co., 1961.

21   *REFLECTIONS ON A MARINE VENUS: A COMPANION
        TO THE LANDSCAPE OF RHODES*. London: Faber
        & Faber, 1953. Illustrated.

        ---. New York: E. P. Dutton, 1960.
        [Issued together with *Prospero's Cell*
        (see A.11).]

        ---. London: Faber & Faber, 1960. Paper-
        back.

        ---. *Venus et la Mer*. Paris: Buchet-
        Chastel, 1962. Translated by Roger Giroux.

        ---. *Leuchtende Orangen. Rhodos, Insel
        des Helios*. Hamburg: Rowholt Verlag,
        1964.

        ---. Hamburg: Rowholt Verlag, 1968.
        Paperback.

        ---. *An Index*, by John Talbot White.
        Edinburgh: The Tragara Press, 1968. [75
        copies for private distribution.]

        ---. London: Faber & Faber, 1978. Paper-
        back. [A new jacket by David Gentleman
        appeared on the paperback edition.]

        ---. New York: Penguin Books, 1978.
        Paperback.

[The Dorset County Library once advertised for "The Submarine Venus."]

22   *PRIVATE DRAFTS*. Nicosia, Cyprus: The Proodos Press, 1955. [3 1/2 x 2 5/8 inches. 100 copies privately printed, signed by the author.]

23   *THE TREE OF IDLENESS AND OTHER POEMS*. London: Faber & Faber, 1955.

24   *SELECTED POEMS*. London: Faber & Faber, 1956.

      ---. New York: Grove Press, 1956. [The British sheets. Published in wrappers, also in blue-black cloth with dust-jacket, as *Evergreen Books of Poetry (E-57)*. Also an edition limited to 100 copies in brown half-cloth and gray boards, with a *justification de tirage* tipped in before p. 7.]

24a   *SELECTED POEMS, 1935-1963*. London: Faber & Faber, 1964. Paperback. ["This new paperback edition of Lawrence Durrell's poetry contains the whole of *Selected Poems*, which was published in 1956 and is now out of print, together with a number of additional poems, of which some are of more recent date and a few have not previously been published in book form."]

      ---. *Poemes (choix de)*. Paris: Gallimard, 1966. Translated by Alain Bosquet.

24b   *SELECTED POEMS*. Selected and with an Introduction by Alan Ross. London: Faber & Faber, 1977.

25   *BITTER LEMONS*. London: Faber & Faber, 1957. Illustrated. [The advance proof

is entitled *Bitter Lemons of Cyprus.*
"Yes, title changed on advice of V. S.
Pritchett for Book Society Choice." The
plates were used to publish an edition
for The Book Society. This imprint follows that of Faber & Faber on the title
page; the inside front flap of the jacket
states "The Book Society Choice for
July," and the price is 16/-. The top
edges of this printing are stained lemon
yellow; on the *verso* of the t.p. appears
(top) in italics: "This edition issued on
first publication by / The Book Society
Ltd in associaton with / Faber and Faber
Ltd / July 1957." No plate changes are
recorded.]

———. London: Readers Union and Faber &
Faber, Ltd., 1958. [Knerr's note, reproduced in the UCLA *Checklist* (see section
H, 1961), indicates that the plates of
the Faber first edition were used to
print copies for The Book Society and
for the Readers Union. However, t.p.
verso of the Readers Union copy reads,
in part, "the book has been reset in 11
point Joanna, and printed by The Aldine
Press, Letchworth."]

———. New York: E. P. Dutton, 1958.

———. London: Faber & Faber, 1959. Paperback. [At a later date, Schweppes circu-
lated copies of the paperback edition as
an advertisement for their "Bitter Lemon"
drink!]

[*N.B.* In 1957, Faber & Faber published *Justine*,
White Eagles Over Serbia, *Bitter Lemons*, and
Esprit de Corps - in that order. This is different from the order we have given, but, as
the numbering of this bibliography has been

quoted elsewhere, we have not risked confusion
by changing it.]

    ---. *Citrons Acides.* Paris: Buchet-
Chastel, 1961. Translated by Roger
Giroux.

    ---. *Bittere Limonen. Erlebtes Cypern.*
Hamburg: Rowholt Verlag, 1962. Translated by Gerda von Uslar.

    ---. Hamburg: Rowholt Verlag, 1967.
Paperback.

26   *ESPRIT DE CORPS: SKETCHES FROM DIPLOMATIC
LIFE.* Illustrated by V. H. Drummond.
London: Faber & Faber, 1957. *"Written
in hopes of making a little money from
Punch (I was 'in extremis'). Submitted
as a book and rejected 'in toto'! The
dear old British sense of Humour at work
again! On publication had numerous fan-
letters from prolapsed ancients who
(subscribers to Punch) thought it was in
the tradition."*

    ---. London: Faber & Faber, 1961. Paper-
back.

    ---. New York: E. P. Dutton, 1968.
Illustrated by Vasiliu. [The Dutton
edition has two sketches not in the
English edition: "La Valise" and "Cry
Wolf."]

27   *JUSTINE: A NOVEL.* London: Faber & Faber,
1957. *"1st edition had about 250 errors,
which were put right in the 2nd, though
some caused beautiful muck-ups in the
French translation, notably 'her tree'
for 'her knee.'. . ."*

———. New York: E. P. Dutton, 1957.

———. Paris: Buchet-Chastel, 1957.
Translated by Roger Giroux.

———. Hamburg: Rowholt Verlag, 1958.
Translated by Maria Carlsson.

———. London: Faber & Faber, 1961.
Paperback.

———. Berlin: Deutsche Buchgemeinschaft,
1962. [Book-club edition.]

———. *Justine. Balthazar. Zwei Romane.*
Zürich: Buchclub Ex Libris, 1962.

———. *Justine.* Hamburg: Deutscher
Bücherbund, 1963. [Book-club edition.]

———. Hamburg: Rowholt Verlag, 1965.
Paperback.

———. Bath: C. Chivers, 1978. [A large
print edition.]

———. Franklin Center, Pennsylvania:
Franklin Library, 1980. Illustrated by
David Palladini. ["Privately printed
and individually signed by the author."]

28 *WHITE EAGLES OVER SERBIA.* London: Faber
& Faber, 1957. [A note in a presentation
copy: *"Purely as a curiosity. I decided
in Yugoslavia to resign and make some
dough out of 12 detective stories which
I had planned - but I was puzzled I
couldn't sell it. Much later I showed
it to Faber. 'A juvenile' they shouted
in a high pitched tone. The trouble was
it was mental age 12: I thought detective stories were about that age - but*

*no: they are nearer age 15 apparently.
Anyway!*
   *"Some snatches of landscape not too
bad - all accurate - and the story
founded on a true recital I'll tell you
about one day."*]

---. New York: Criterion Books, 1957.

---. London: Chatto & Windus, 1961.
Edited and abridged by G. A. Verdin.

---. London: Faber & Faber, 1962.
Paperback.

---. New York: Avon Camelot, 1966.
Paperback.

---. *Weisse Adler Ueber Serbien.   Ein
Abenteuerroman für jugendliche Leser.*
Hamburg: Rowholt Verlag, 1966.   Trans-
lated by Christian Spiel.   Paperback.

---. Harmondsworth, Middlesex: Penguin
Books, 1980. ["A Peacock book in
association with Faber & Faber."]

29   *BALTHAZAR: A NOVEL.*   London: Faber &
Faber, 1958.

---. New York: E. P. Dutton, 1958.

---. Paris: Buchet-Chastel, 1959.
Translated by Roger Giroux.

---. Hamburg: Rowholt Verlag, 1959.
Translated by Gerda von Uslar and Maria
Carlsson.

---. London: Faber & Faber, 1961.   Paperback.

---. Berlin: Deutsche Buchgemeinschaft,
1962. [Book-club edition.]

---. *Justine. Balthazar. Zwei Romane.*
Zürich: Buchclub Ex Libris, 1962.

---. *Balthazar.* Hamburg: Deutscher
Bücherbund, 1963. [Book-club edition.]

---. Hamburg: Rowholt Verlag, 1965.
Paperback.

30   *MOUNTOLIVE: A NOVEL.* London: Faber &
Faber, 1958.

---. New York: E. P. Dutton, 1958.

---. Hamburg: Rowholt Verlag, 1960.
Translated by Maria Carlsson and Gerda
von Uslar.

---. Paris: Buchet-Chastel, 1961.
Translated by Roger Giroux.

---. London: Faber & Faber, 1961.
Paperback.

---. Berlin: Deutsche Buchgemeinschaft,
1962. [Book-club edition.]

---. Hamburg: Deutscher Bücherbund,
1963. [Book-club edition.]

---. *Mountolive. Clea. Zwei Romane.*
Zürich: Buchclub Ex Libris, 1963.

---. *Mountolive.* Hamburg: Rowholt Verlag,
1965. Paperback.

31   *STIFF UPPER LIP: LIFE AMONG THE DIPLOMATS.*
"Nicolas Bentley drew the pictures."
London: Faber & Faber, 1958.

———. New York: E. P. Dutton, 1959.

[The Faber edition contains "La Valise" and "Cry Wolf," which are not in the Dutton edition (but see A.26), while the Dutton edition contains "A Smircher Smirched," which is not in the Faber edition.]

———. London: Faber & Faber, 1966. Paperback.

32   *ART AND OUTRAGE: A CORRESPONDENCE ABOUT HENRY MILLER BETWEEN ALFRED PERLES AND LAWRENCE DURRELL. (With an intermission by Henry Miller.)* Portrait. London: Putnam, 1959.

———. New York: E. P. Dutton, 1961.

———. *Kunst und Provokation. Ein Briefwechsel.* Hamburg: Rowholt Verlag, 1960. Translated by Kurt Wagenseil.

———. London: Village Press, 1973. Paperback.

33   *CLEA: A NOVEL.* London: Faber & Faber, 1960.

———. New York: E. P. Dutton, 1960.

———. Paris: Buchet-Chastel, 1960. Translated by Roger Giroux.

———. London: Faber & Faber, 1961. Paperback.

———. Hamburg: Rowholt Verlag, 1961. Translated by Walter Schürenberg.

———. Berlin: Deutsche Buchgemeinschaft,

1962. [Book-club edition.]

---. Hamburg: Deutscher Bücherbund,
1963. [Book-club edition.]

---. *Mountolive. Clea. Zwei Romane.*
Zürich: Buchclub Ex Libris, 1963.

---. *Clea.* Hamburg: Rowholt Verlag,
1965. Paperback.

33a   *THE ALEXANDRIA QUARTET: JUSTINE, BALTHA-
ZAR, MOUNTOLIVE, CLEA. With numerous
revisions in the text and a new Preface.*
London: Faber & Faber, 9 November 1962.
[Limited to 500 copies signed by the
author. Also ordinary trade edition.]

---. New York: E. P. Dutton, 4 December
1962. [Dutton's signed limited edition
consisted of 199 copies for distribution
in the United States in addition to the
500 copies distributed by Faber. Faber
printed both editions but gave Dutton
their own imprint and other necessary
alterations in the prelims. Dutton
produced their own binding, their own box,
and also their own endpapers. Also
ordinary trade edition.]

---. *Le Quatuor d'Alexandrie.* Paris:
Buchet-Chastel, 1963. Translated by
Roger Giroux.

---. *Das Alexandria-Quartett.* Hamburg:
Rowholt Verlag, 1977. [Softcover only.]

[An order for *The Alexandria Quartet*,
sent to one of England's leading bookshops,
was passed to the music department!]

34   *COLLECTED POEMS.* London: Faber & Faber,
1960.

34a   *THE POETRY OF LAWRENCE DURRELL.* New York:
      E. P. Dutton, 1962. [Substantially
      different from the Faber *Collected Poems*
      of 1960, the order of the poems being the
      same, but many having been omitted.]

34b   *COLLECTED POEMS. New and revised edition.*
      London: Faber & Faber, 1968.

      ---. New York: E. P. Dutton, 1968.

34c   *COLLECTED POEMS, 1931-1974.* Edited by
      James A. Brigham. London: Faber & Faber,
      1980.

      ---. New York: Viking, 1980.

      ---. London: Bernard Stone at The Turret
      Bookshop, 1980. *Therpewin Poetry Series
      No. 1.* With an etching by Henry Moore.
      [Limited to 100 copies signed by artist
      and author, with an etching signed by the
      artist. Endpapers designed by Henry Moore
      and dedicated to L.D. Bound in full oasis
      goatskin by W. T. Morell of Covent Garden.
      Handsewn on cords with handsewn silk head-
      bands. Five raised bands on spine, hand-
      lettered and hand-tooled with an original
      design by Henry Moore created specifically
      for this edition. In white art canvas
      slipcase. The price of this limited
      edited was £750.]

35   *BRIEFWECHSEL UBER ACTIS.* With Gustaf
      Gründgens. Hamburg: Rowholt Verlag, 1961.
      Wrappers. Frontispiece. [Apparently
      produced by Rowholt for private distribu-
      tion: there is no entry for this item in
      the German national bibliographies,
      although the National Union Catalogue does
      list a copy. (See A.19 for Durrell's
      comments on the production of *Sappho*, and

also Section F, *Die Zeit* (24 November
1961), and Section H, *Theater Heute*
(1962).]

35a   *GRODDECK*. Wiesbaden: Limes-Verlag, 1961.
Translated by Grete Weil. [A translation,
with some slight changes, of Durrell's
"Studies in Genius, VI: Groddeck," which
was first published in *Horizon* (1948);
see Section E.]

36   *THE FIFTH ANTIQUARIAN BOOK FAIR: HANDLIST
OF EXHIBITORS*. London: National Book
League and Antiquarian Booksellers'
Association, June 1962. Wrappers.
[3 1/2 x 8 1/8 inches. Contains an
introductory essay on book collecting.
In addition to the ordinary edition,
which was distributed gratis, one copy
was printed on pink handmade paper for
Lawrence Durrell and ten copies on Barcham
Green handmade paper, signed by Durrell;
the latter were auctioned in aid of the
Antiquarian Booksellers' Benevolent Fund.
Reprinted in *The Antiquarian Bookman*
(New York) (May-June 1962).]

37   *LAWRENCE DURRELL AND HENRY MILLER: A
PRIVATE CORRESPONDENCE*. Edited by George
Wickes. New York: E. P. Dutton, 1963.

---. London: Faber & Faber, 1963.
[Publication of the American edition
preceded that of the English edition by
a few weeks.]

[Two pages of text were omitted from the
subsequent American edition.]

---. *Une Correspondance Privée*. Paris:
Buchet-Chastel, 1963. Translated by
Bernard Willerval.

---. *Briefe*. Hamburg: Rowholt Verlag, 1967. Translated by Herbert Zand.

38   *BECCAFICO/LE BECFIGUE*. Montpellier: La Licorne, 1963. English text together with a translation into French by F.-J. Temple. Wrappers. [150 copies privately printed on pink paper, signed by the author. 6 1/4 x 4 3/4 inches.]

39   *A PERSIAN LADY*. [Edinburgh]: The Tragara Press, August 1963. [Folio broadsheet. Limited to 6 copies.]

40   *AN IRISH FAUSTUS: A MORALITY IN NINE SCENES*. London: Faber & Faber, 1963.

---. *Ein Irischer Faust: Schauspiel in neun Bildern*. Hamburg: Rowholt Verlag, 1963. Translated by Ursula Schuh. [This is the German acting edition. For the trade edition, see A.19. A number of changes were suggested for the German version by Oscar Fritz Schuh, who directed the production at the Deutsches Schauspielhaus, Hamburg, in 1963. The final scene, especially, differs considerably from the English text; for an analysis, see Section H, Hoops (1976).]

---. *An Irish Faustus*. New York: E. P. Dutton, 1964.

---. *Un Faust Irlandais: moralité en neuf scènes*. Paris: Gallimard, 1974. Translated by F.-J. Temple. Wrappers.

41   *LA DESCENTE DU STYX*. Traduit de l'Anglais par F.-J. Temple et suivi du Texte Original. Montpellier: La Murène, 1964. Wrappers. [4to. 250 copies privately printed and signed by the author.]

---. Preface by F.-J. Temple. Santa
Barbara, Calif.: The Capricorn Press,
1971. [Cover by Durrell. Limited and
ordinary editions.]

41a *EXHIBITION OF PAINTINGS BY OSCAR EPFS*
[Lawrence Durrell]. Paris: 1964. [Was
there a catalogue or poster? *"Not really.
A few typed sheets with titles. 200
copies of a hand-painted poster, half by
me and half by Nadia Blokh, were carried
round and placed in the indulgent bars
and bistros of the Latin quarter by Epfs
and his wife and two artloving girl
friends."*]

42 *ACTE: A PLAY*. London: Faber & Faber,
1964. [With 4 photographs of the production in German mounted by Gustaf Gründgens
at the Deutsches Schauspielhaus, Hamburg,
November 1961. For German acting text,
see Section H, *Theater Heute* (1962).]

---. New York: E. P. Dutton, 1965.

---. *Actis: Drama in drei Akten*. Hamburg:
Rowholt Verlag, 1965. Translated by
Robert Schnorr. [This is the German
acting edition. For the first appearance
of the German text, see Section H, *Theater
Heute* (1962); for the German trade
edition, see A.19.]

43 *SAUVE QUI PEUT*. "Nicolas Bentley drew
the pictures." London: Faber & Faber,
1966.

---. New York: E. P. Dutton, 1967.

44 *THE IKONS AND OTHER POEMS*. London:
Faber & Faber, 1966.

---. New York: E. P. Dutton, 1967.

---. Redding Ridge, Conn.: Black Swan
Books, 1981. Illustrated. [A newly
typeset edition with photographs.]

44a   *ESPRIT DE CORPS, ODER, DIPLOMATEN UNTER
SICH*. Hamburg: Rowholt Verlag, 1968.
Translated by Susanne Lepsius. Illustrated
by Nicolas Bentley. [This is not a
translation of *Esprit de Corps* (1957) but
a selection from it and from *Stiff Upper
Lip* (1958) and *Sauve Qui Peut* (1966).
Although none of these illustrations,
commissioned by Rowholt, appeared in any
edition in English until 1974 (see A.53),
they are to be found in the following
edition in Dutch.]

---. *Esprit de Corps: Diplomaten onder
elkaar*. Netherlands: Ke Boekerij nv
Baarn, [n.d.].

---. *Esprit de Corps, oder, Diplomaten
unter sich*. Hamburg: Rowholt Verlag,
1976.

45   *TUNC: A NOVEL*. London: Faber & Faber,
1968.

---. New York: E. P. Dutton, 1968.

---. London: Faber & Faber, 1969.
Paperback.

---. Paris: Gallimard, 1969. Translated
by Roger Giroux.

---. Hamburg: Rowholt Verlag, 1969.
Translated by Susanne Lepsius.

---. New York: Pocket Books, 1970.
Paperback.

---.   Hamburg: Rowholt Verlag, 1972.
Paperback.

---.   New York: Penguin Books, 1979.
Paperback.

46   *SPIRIT OF PLACE: LETTERS AND ESSAYS ON
TRAVEL.*   Edited by Alan G. Thomas.
London: Faber & Faber, 1969.
[8 illustrations after paintings by
Durrell.]

---.   New York: E. P. Dutton, 1969.

---.   London: Faber & Faber, 1971.
Paperback.

---,   New York: E. P. Dutton, 1971.
Paperback.

47   *NUNQUAM: A NOVEL.*   London: Faber & Faber,
1970.

---.   New York: E. P. Dutton, 1970.

---.   Paris: Gallimard, 1970.   Translated
by Roger Giroux.

---.   Hamburg: Rowholt Verlag, 1970.
Translated by Susanne Lepsius.

---.   London: Faber & Faber, 1971.
Paperback.

---.   New York: Pocket Books, 1971.
Paperback.

---.   Hamburg: Rowholt Verlag, 1973.
Paperback.

---.   New York: Penguin Books, 1979.
Paperback.

47a   *THE REVOLT OF APHRODITE*. London: Faber
       & Faber, 1974. [*Tunc* and *Nunquam* in one
       volume. In terms of bookmaking, a bit
       of a shotgun marriage.]

48   *FAUSTUS: A POEM*. London [n.p.], 1970.
       [Text in facsimile of Durrell's hand-
       writing. Folding card, colored cover
       also designed by Durrell. Limited to
       50 numbered copies signed by Durrell
       (plus a very few out of series).]

49   *THE RED LIMBO LINGO: A POETRY NOTEBOOK*.
       London: Faber & Faber, 1971. [100
       copies signed by Durrell. Also 500
       ordinary copies.]

       ---. New York: E. P. Dutton, 1971.
       [100 copies signed by Durrell. Also 500
       ordinary copies.]

50   *ON THE SUCHNESS OF THE OLD BOY*. London:
       Turret Books, 1972. Drawings by Sappho
       Durrell. **Pictured wrappers.** [Small
       folio. 226 copies: i.e., 26 lettered
       copies not for sale, and 200 numbered
       copies signed by the poet and the
       artist.]

50a   *LE GRAND SUPPOSITOIRE: ENTRETIENS AVEC
       MARC ALYN*. Paris: Pierre Belfond, 1972.
       [Contains an essay by Marc Alyn, a long
       taped conversation with Durrell, an
       horoscopic interpretative portrait of
       Durrell by Conrad Moricand (who figures
       in Miller's *Devil in Paradise*), and notes
       and reflections by Durrell.]

       ---. *The Big Supposer: A Dialogue with
       Marc Alyn*. London: Abelard-Schuman,
       1973. Translated by Francine Barker.

---. New York: Grove Press, 1975.
Translated by Francine Barker.

51 *VEGA AND OTHER POEMS*. London: Faber &
Faber, 1973.

---. Woodstock, N.Y.: The Overlook
Press, 1973.

---. London: Faber & Faber, 1974.
Paperback.

51a *THE HAPPY ROCK*. London: Village Press,
1973. Paperback [?]. [First published
in *The Happy Rock* (1945); see Section D.]

51b *THE PLANT-MAGIC MAN*. Santa Barbara,
Calif.: Capra Press, February 1973.
[Besides the regular, paper edition,
"two hundred numbered copies, signed by
the author, were handbound by Earle
Gray." Appeared previously in the *New
York Herald Tribune* and *Midi Libre*.]

52 *MONSIEUR, OR THE PRINCE OF DARKNESS*.
London: Faber & Faber, 1974.

---. New York: Viking Press, 1975 [i.e.,
1974. Though containing the statement
"published in 1975," it actually appeared
in late 1974. The American edition lacks
the subtitle.]

---. London: Faber & Faber, 1975.
Paperback.

---. New York: Pocket Books, 1976.
Paperback.

---. *Monsieur, oder der Fürst der
Finsternis*. Hamburg: Rowholt Verlag,
1977.

53   *THE BEST OF ANTROBUS*. London: Faber &
        Faber, 1974. "Nicolas Bentley drew the
        pictures." [The twenty best Antrobus
        stories. Contains three new drawings by
        Nicolas Bentley and five which he made
        for the German edition published by
        Rowholt (see A.44a), together with a
        jacket picture by him.]

54   *LIFELINES*. Edinburgh: The Tragara Press,
        December 1974. [Limited to 115 copies,
        hand-printed. Contains "Certain Land-
        falls," "Postmark," "Picture of Geishas,"
        and "A Patch of Dust."]

54a   *BLUE THIRST*. Santa Barbara, Calif.:
        Capra Press, February 1975. Illustrated.
        [Slightly edited transcripts of two
        lectures given in California: "Blue
        Thirst" and "Propaganda and Impropaganda."
        Illustrated with photographs of Durrell,
        Miller, Katsimbalis, and others. Besides
        the regular, paper edition, "250 numbered
        copies, signed by the author, were hand-
        bound by Emily Paine."]

55   *SICILIAN CAROUSEL*. London: Faber &
        Faber, 1977. Illustrated.

        ———. New York: Viking Press, 1977.

        ———. New York: Penguin Books, 1978.
        Paperback.

56   *THE GREEK ISLANDS*. London: Faber &
        Faber, 1978. Illustrated. [4to. Color
        and other plates. Durrell's entry in
        the 1978-1979 edition of *Who's Who* lists
        A Treasury of Greek Islands.]

        ———. New York: Viking Press, 1978.

---. *Griechische Inseln*. Hamburg:
Rowholt Verlag, 1978. Translated by
Edwin Ortmann.

---. *The Greek Islands*. New York:
Penguin Books, 1980. Paperback.

57   *LIVIA, OR BURIED ALIVE*. London: Faber
& Faber, 1978.

---. New York: Viking Press, 1979.

---. *Livia, oder lebendig begraben*.
Hamburg: Rowholt Verlag, 1980. Translated
by Susanne Lepsius.

58   *A SMILE IN THE MIND'S EYE*. London:
Wildwood House, 1980. [Includes "Tao
and Its Glozes," from *The Aryan Path*
(1939); see Section E.]

B. TRANSLATIONS

1   *SIX POEMS FROM THE GREEK OF SEKILIANOS AND SEFERIS*. Rhodes [n.p.], 1946. Wrappers. [Contains note signed "L. D.". *"Fifty copies I think."*]

1a   See Section E: *The New English Weekly*, XV (28 September 1939).

1b   See Section E: *Seven*, No. 7 (Christmas 1939).

1c   See Section E: *Bulletin of the John Rylands Library* (1942).

2   *THE KING OF ASINE AND OTHER POEMS*, by George Seferis. Translated from the Greek by Bernard Spencer, Nanos Valaoritis, Lawrence Durrell. London: John Lehmann, 1948. With an Introduction by Rex Warner.

2a   See Section E: *Penguin New Writing*, No. 33 (1948).

3   *THE CURIOUS HISTORY OF POPE JOAN*. Translated out of the modern Greek of Emmanuel Royidis by Lawrence Durrell, and illustrated by John Buckland-Wright. London: Rodney Phillips & Green, 1948. [13 illustrations. Demy 8vo; 9 3/4 x

6 1/8 inches; pp. i-xxiv, 1-134. Never
issued. The firm of publishers who
planned it went out of business before
the book could be produced. Three sets
of proofs have survived. There was also
to have been an edition limited to 150 on
moldmade paper. Copies survive of a
Prospectus bearing one of the illustrations.]

———. London: Derek Verschoyle, 1954.
[Frontispiece only.]

———. London: Andre Deutsch, 1960.
[Revised edition with new preface but no
frontispiece.]

———. New York: E. P. Dutton, 1961.

———. London: Consul Books, World
Distributors, 1962. Paperback.

———. London: Sphere Books, 1971.
Paperback.

———. Woodstock, N.Y.: The Overlook Press,
1972.

———. New York: Penguin Books, 1974.
[Set by a photoreduction process from the
plates of the Overlook Press edition.]

3a See Section E: *London Magazine*, I: 9
(October 1954).

3b See Section E.: *London Magazine*, III: 7
(July 1956).

4 *SELECTED POEMS* by Alain Bosquet.
Translated by Wallace Fowlie, Lawrence
Durrell, Samuel Beckett, and Jean and
Elisabeth Malaquais. [n.p.:] Ohio

University, 1971[?]. [Contains ten poems
translated by Durrell.]

5   *THREE POEMS OF CAVAFY*. Edinburgh: The
Tragara Press, 1980. [Edition limited
to 95 copies.]

C. PREFACES

1   Stephanides, Theodore. *CLIMAX IN CRETE*.
     London: Faber & Faber, 1946. Maps.

1a   Gotch, Paul. *THREE CARAVAN CITIES: PETRA,
     JERASH, BAALBEK, AND ST. CATHERINE'S
     MONASTERY, SINAI*. Alexandria: Whitehead
     Morris Egypt, 1945.

1b   Georghiou, Georgios Pol. *AN EXHIBITION
     OF PAINTINGS* [n.d.]. [A catalogue of the
     Cypriot painter's work shown in Athens.
     *"I did a general article on him in the
     Cyprus Review* (April 1955) *with pics,
     and he used it afterwards as a catalogue
     blurb* (in Greek)."]

2   Nin, Anaïs. *CHILDREN OF THE ALBATROSS*.
     London: Peter Owen, 1959. [The New York
     edition (E. P. Dutton, 1947) does not
     contain the preface.]

3   Venezis, Ilias. *AEOLIA*. London: William
     Campion, 1949. Translated by E. D.
     Scott-Kilvert.

     ---. *Beyond the Aegean*. New York: The
     Vanguard Press [1956?]. Translated by
     E. D. Scott-Kilvert.

4   Tremayne, Penelope. *BELOW THE TIDE*.

London: Hutchinson, 1958.

---. Boston: Houghton Mifflin, 1959.

5   Guirdham, Arthur. *CHRIST AND FREUD: A STUDY OF RELIGIOUS EXPERIENCE AND OBSERVANCE*. London: George Allen & Unwin, 1959. [In a review entitled "Couch-Bound Christians," the *Irish Times* printed the title as *Christ and Friend*. *"Too good to change!!!"*]

6   *A HENRY MILLER READER*. Edited with an Introduction by Lawrence Durrell. New York: New Directions, 1959.

---. *The Best of Henry Miller*. London: Heinemann, 1960.

---. *Ein Henry Miller Lesebuch*. Hamburg: Rowholt Verlag, 1961. Translated by Carl Bach and others.

---. Hamburg: Rowholt Verlag, 1971. Paperback.

7   Wideson, Reno. *PORTRAIT OF CYPRUS*. The Hague, Deppo Holland: [privately printed, n.d. (1961)]. [Edition limited to 25 numbered copies, signed by Durrell.]

8   Groddeck, Georg. *DAS BUCH VOM ES: PSYCHOANALYTISCHER BRIEFWECHSEL MIT EINER FREUNDIN*. Verwort von Lawrence Durrell. Wiesbaden: Limes-Verlag, 1961.

---. *The Book of the It*. New York: Random House, 1961.

---. *Das Buch vom Es*. München: Kindler-Verlag, 1968. Paperback.

9   Brandt, Bill. *PERSPECTIVE OF NUDES*.
    London: The Bodley Head, 1961. [4to.
    90 photographs. English edition
    distributed in America by Amphoto Ltd.]

10 Nimr [Smart], Amy. *AN EXHIBITION OF
    PAINTINGS*. Paris: Gallerie de Marignan,
    5-27 May 1961. [Preface in French.]

11 Rouff, Marcel. *THE PASSIONATE EPICURE*.
    London: Faber & Faber, 1961. Translated
    by Claude [Mrs. Lawrence Durrell].
    Illustrated by Charles Mozley.

11a Miller, Henry. *SEXUS*. New York: Grove
    Press, 1962.

    ---. New York: Grove Press, 1965.
    Paperback.

11b Seignolle, Claude. *UN CORBEAU DE TOUTES
    COULEURS*. Paris: Editions Denoël, 1962.

12 Stark, Freya. *THE JOURNEY'S ECHO: A
    SELECTION*. London: John Murray, 1963.
    Illustrated.

13 Blokh, Nadia. *AN EXHIBITION OF
    PAINTINGS*. Paris: [n.p.], 1963.
    [Preface, in French, to a catalogue.]

14 *LEAR'S CORFU: AN ANTHOLOGY DRAWN FROM THE
    PAINTER'S LETTERS BY MARIA ASPIOTI*.
    Corfu: Corfu Travel, 1965. Wrappers.
    [4to. 8 views of Corfu reproduced from
    Lear's lithographs.]

15 Peyre, Marc. *CAPTIVE OF ZOUR*. London:
    Alan Ross, 1966. Translated by Claude.

16 Douglas, Keith. *ALAMEIN TO ZEM ZEM*.
    London: Faber & Faber, 1966.

---. New York: Chilmark Press, 1966.

17   Seignolle, Claude. *THE ACCURSED (Les Malédictions)*. London: George Allen & Unwin, 1966. [French edition published by G. P. Maisonneuve et Larose, Paris.]

18   Miller, Henry. *ORDER AND CHAOS CHEZ HANS REICHEL*. Tucson, Ariz.: Loujon Press, 1966. [Cork edition of 1,399 copies. Leather edition of 99 copies, signed and dated. Leather edition of 26 copies, signed, dated and lettered by the author from "A" to "Z," the autograph page inscribed to the collector.]

19   *100 GREAT BOOKS: MASTERPIECES OF ALL TIME*. London: Odhams Books Limited, 1966. Edited by John Canning.

20   Gordon, William A. *THE MIND AND ART OF HENRY MILLER*. Baton Rouge: Louisiana State University Press, 1967.

---. London: Jonathan Cape, 1968.

21   Gaussen, Ivan. *SOMMIERES: PROMENADE A TRAVERS SON PASSE*. Sommières: [n.p.], 1968. [50 copies signed by both Gaussen and Durrell.]

22   Lawrence, David Herbert. *LADY CHATTERLEY'S LOVER*. New York: Bantam Books, 1968. Paperback.

22a   Thomas, Dylan. *OEUVRES COMPLETS*. Paris: Editions du Seuil, 1970.

23   Lewis, Percy Wyndham. *TARR*. Paris: Christian Bourgois, 1971. [First French edition.]

23a   Sykes, Gerald. *THE PERENNIAL AVANTGARDE*. Englewood Cliffs, N.J.: Prentice-Hall, 1971.

24   Temple, F.-J. *FOGHORN: POEMS*. Santa Barbara, Calif.: The Capricorn Press, 1971. Translated by Naomi Green. "Designed & printed March 1971 / by Noel Young in Santa Barbara / for the Capricorn Press. This edition / is limited to 750 softcover copies / & 100 copies handbound by / Earle Gray, numbered / & signed by the poet."

25   Wordsworth, William. *POEMS*. Harmondsworth, Middlesex: Penguin Books, 1972. Selected and edited by Durrell.

26   Lawrence, David Herbert. *ETRUSCAN PLACES*. London: The Folio Society, 1972. Photographs by Leonard von Matt.

26a   *PEN AS PENCIL: DRAWINGS AND PAINTINGS BY BRITISH AUTHORS*. London: The National Book League, in co-operation with The British Council, 1973. [Catalog of an exhibition at International Culture Center, Antwerp (6 October – 4 November 1973) and at The Royal Library, Brussels (1 December 1973 – 26 January 1974. Also contains a list of sketches and prints by Durrell in the Exhibition.]

27   Lacarriére, Jacques. *THE GNOSTICS*. London: Peter Owen, 1977 [1973].

28   Daniells, Anthony. *UZES EN DESSINS*. Flaux, France: [n.p.], 1978. [Oblong 4to. 28 plates. Preface in French and in English. First ten copies contained the misprint "sophistification;" this was 'corrected' to "sophitication."]

29   Gascoyne, David. *PARIS JOURNAL 1937-1939*.
      London: Enitharmon Press, 1978. [Also
      contains introductory poem by Durrell,
      "Journal, to David Gascoyne" (see Section
      E: *The New English Weekly*, XV: 21). Also
      a limited edition of 75 copies, signed by
      the author, printed on yellow laid paper,
      bound in half linen and marbled boards.]

30   Daniels, Robin. *CONVERSATIONS WITH
      MENUHIN*. London: MacDonald and James,
      1979. Illustrated.

      ---. New York: St. Martin's Press, 1980.
      Illustrated.

31   Burn, A. R. and M. *THE LIVING PAST OF
      GREECE*. London: Herbert Press, 1980.

      ---. Boston: Little, Brown and Company,
      1980.

32   *RETURN TO OASIS: WAR POEMS AND
      RECOLLECTIONS FROM THE MIDDLE EAST,
      1940-1946*. Edited by Victor Selwyn, Erik
      de Mauny, Ian Fletcher, G. S. Fraser and
      John Waller. Consultants Tambimuttu and
      John Cromer. London: Shepheard-Walwyn,
      1980. "With 3 maps, 2 contemporary JON
      cartoons, 2 black-and-white and 1 full
      colour Keith Douglas drawings." [Also
      contains John Braun, "Lawrence Durrell's
      Arrival at Alexandria."]

D. CONTRIBUTIONS TO BOOKS

1   *MASTERPIECE OF THRILLS.* [Edited by John
Gawsworth.] London: Daily Express [n.d.
1936?]. Contains "The Cherries." [See
D.45a.]

2   *PROEMS.* Edited by Oswell Blakeston.
London: The Fortune Press, 1938.
Contains "Uncebuncke / A Biography in
Little;" "Five Soliloquies Upon the
Tomb," and selections from "Themes
Heraldic." [This is not the first
appearance of Durrell's poems in book
form, as the prefatory note erroneously
claims.]

3   *NEW DIRECTIONS IN PROSE & POETRY 1939.*
Edited by James Laughlin IV. Norfolk,
Conn.: New Directions, 1939. Contains
"Gracie," a selection from *The Black Book,*
with an introduction by Laughlin. [This
is the first publication of any part of
The Black Book in America. Prefaced by
.a lengthy editor's note praising Durrell
and recommending purchase of the book
"through your Paris bookseller."]

4   *NEW DIRECTIONS IN PROSE & POETRY 1940.*
Edited by James Laughlin IV. Norfolk,
Conn.: New Directions, 1940. Contains
"Poem in Space and Time;" "A Noctuary;"
"Self," and "At Corinth."

37

5 *DAYLIGHT/EUROPEAN ARTS & LETTERS/*
   YESTERDAY TODAY TOMORROW. London: The
   Hogarth Press, 1941. Contains translation,
   with George Katsimbalis, of George
   Seferis, "Myth of Our History."

6 Miller, Henry. *THE COLOSSUS OF MAROUSSI*.
   San Francisco: The Colt Press, 1941.

   ---. Special edition on better paper.
   [Limited to 100 copies signed by Miller.
   *"Regular edition did not exceed 1,500
   copies."*]

   ---. London: Secker & Warburg, 1942.

   ---. *Der Koloss von Maroussi: Eine Reise
   nach Griechenland*. Hamburg: Rowholt
   Verlag, 1956. Translated by Carl Bach
   and Lola Humm-Sernau.

   ---. *The Colossus of Maroussi*. New
   York: New Directions, 1958. Paperback.

   ---. *Der Koloss von Maroussi*.
   Dusseldorf: Deutscher Bücherbund, 1960.

   ---. Hamburg: Rowholt Verlag, 1965.

   ---. Hamburg: Rowholt Verlag, 1978.

6a *A LITTLE BOOK OF MODERN VERSE*. Edited by
   Anne Ridler, with a Preface by T. S. Eliot.
   London: Faber & Faber, November 1941.
   Contains "In a Time of Crisis."

7 *THE FORTUNE ANTHOLOGY*. London: The
   Fortune Press [n.d. 1942]. Contains
   "At Epidaurus."

8 *POETRY IN WARTIME*. Edited by Tambimuttu.
   London: Faber & Faber, 1942. Contains

"Epitaph;" "Island Fugue;" "The Green Man;" "In Time of Crisis," and "Letter to Seferis the Greek."

9   *NEW ROAD 1944/NEW DIRECTIONS IN EUROPEAN ART AND LETTERS.*   Edited by Alex Comfort and John Bayliss.   London: The Grey Walls Press, 1944.   Contains "For a Nursery Mirror."

10   *SELECTED WRITING.*   Edited by Reginald Moore, poetry selected by Tambimuttu. London: Nicholson & Watson, 1944. Contains "On First Looking into the Loeb Horace."   [Two variant bindings.]

10a   *NEW POETRY.*   Edited by Nicholas Moore. London: The Fortune Press, 1944. Contains "This Unimportant Morning" and "Coptic Poem."

11   *PERSONAL LANDSCAPE: AN ANTHOLOGY OF EXILE.*   Compiled by Robin Fedden, Bernard Spencer, and Lawrence Durrell. London: Editions Poetry London, 1945.

12   *THE HAPPY ROCK: A BOOK ABOUT HENRY MILLER* [by numerous writers.]   Berkeley, Calif.: Bern Porter, 1945.   Contains "The Happy Rock," the book's opening essay.

13   *ATLANTIC ANTHOLOGY.*   Edited by Nicholas Moore and Douglas Newton.   Contains "Tribes;" "Sea Music;" "Pearls;" "Air to Syria;" "Heloise and Abelard;" "The Pilot" and "La Rochefoucauld."

14   *NEW WRITING AND DAYLIGHT 1946.*   London: John Lehmann, 1946.   Contains "Blind Homer" and "Rodini," as well as "The Death Feast of the Greeks" by Angelos Sekilianos, translated by Durrell.

14a   *A LITTLE TREASURY OF MODERN POETRY,
ENGLISH AND AMERICAN.* Edited by Oscar
Williams. New York: Charles Scribner's
Sons, 1946. Contains "In a Time of
Crisis" and "A Ballad of the Good Lord
Nelson."

---. Revised edition, 1950. Also
contains "On Seeming to Presume."

---. 3rd edition, 1970. Also contains
"On First Looking into Loeb's Horace."

15   *MIDDLE EAST ANTHOLOGY.* Edited by John
Waller and Erik de Mauny. London:
Lindsay Drummond, 1946. Contains "A
Landmark Gone;" "Alexandria" and "Conon
in Alexandria."

16   *TRAVELLERS' VERSES.* Edited by M. G.
Lloyd Thomas. London: Frederick Muller,
1946. Illustrated by E. Bawden. Contains
"Nemea."

17   *AND SO TO BED: AN ALBUM.* Compiled by
Edward Sackville-West, from the B.B.C.
feature. London: Phoenix House, 1947.
Contains "Corinth" and "On Ithaca
Standing."

17a   *POEMS OF THE WAR YEARS: AN ANTHOLOGY.*
Edited by Maurice Wollman. London:
Macmillan, 1948. Contains "Nemea."

---. London[?]: The Scholar's Library,
1950.

18   *T. S. ELIOT: A SYMPOSIUM.* Compiled by
Richard March and Tambimuttu. London:
Editions Poetry London, 1948. Contains
"Anniversary."

---. Chicago: Henry Regnery Company, 1949.

18a *THE NEW BRITISH POETS*. Edited by Kenneth
Rexroth. Norfolk, Conn.: New Directions,
1949. Contains "Delos;" "Eight Aspects
of Melissa;" "This Unimportant Morning"
and "To Ping-kû, Asleep."

18b *100 MODERN POEMS*. Compiled by Selden
Rodman. New York: Pellegrini & Cudahy,
1949. Contains "A Ballad of the Good
Lord Nelson."

18c *THE PENGUIN BOOK OF CONTEMPORARY VERSE*.
Edited by Kenneth Allott. Harmondsworth,
Middlesex: Penguin Books, 1950. Contains
Carols I, III, and V from "The Death of
General Uncebunke," and "A Ballad of the
Good Lord Nelson."

18d *THE FABER BOOK OF MODERN VERSE*. Edited
by Michael Roberts, with a supplement of
poems chosen by Anne Ridler. London:
Faber & Faber, 1951. Contains "In
Arcadia;" "Coptic Poem;" "Swans;" "Green
Coconuts" and "Water Colour of Venice."
[This is the second edition of *The Faber
Book of Modern Verse*; the first edition
contained no poems by Durrell.]

18e *A LITTLE TREASURY OF BRITISH POETRY*.
Edited by Oscar Williams. New York:
Charles Scribner's Sons, 1951. Contains
"At Epidaurus."

18f *MODERN POETRY: AMERICAN AND BRITISH*.
Edited by Kimon Friar and John Malcolm
Brinnin. New York: Appleton-Century-
Crofts, 1951. Contains poems and two
author's notes, one answering the question
"Why do I write?" and the other discussing
the Conon figure as a mask.

18g *THE WORLDLY MUSE: AN ANTHOLOGY OF
     SERIOUS LIGHT VERSE*. Edited by A. J. M.
     Smith. New York: Abelard Press, 1951.
     Contains "The Ballad of the Good Lord
     Nelson."

19   *PLEASURES OF NEW WRITING*. Edited by John
     Lehmann. London: John Lehmann, 1952.
     Contains "From a Winter Journal."

19a *IMMORTAL POEMS OF THE ENGLISH LANGUAGE:
     BRITISH AND AMERICAN POETRY FROM CHAUCER'S
     TIME TO THE PRESENT DAY*. Edited by Oscar
     Williams. New York: Washington Square
     Press, 1952. Contains "A Ballad of the
     Good Lord Nelson."

20   *NEW POEMS 1952: A P.E.N. ANTHOLOGY*.
     Edited by Clifford Dyment, Roy Fuller,
     and Montagu Slater. London: Michael
     Joseph, 1952. Contains "Sarajevo."

21   *NEW POEMS 1953: A P.E.N. ANTHOLOGY*.
     Edited by Robert Conquest, Michael
     Hamburger, and Howard Sergeant. London:
     Michael Joseph, 1953. Contains "Clouds
     of Glory" and "Chanel."

21a *AN ANTHOLOGY OF CONTEMPORARY VERSE*.
     Edited by Margaret J. O'Donnell. Glasgow:
     Blackie & Son, 1953. Contains "On Ithaca
     Standing."

21b *THE FABER BOOK OF TWENTIETH CENTURY VERSE:
     AN ANTHOLOGY OF VERSE IN BRITAIN, 1900-
     1950*. Edited by John Heath-Stubbs and
     David Wright. London: Faber & Faber,
     1953. Contains "On Ithaca Standing" and
     "Nemea."

21c *MODERN VERSE, 1900-1950*. Edited by
     Phyllis M. Jones. Oxford: Oxford

University Press, 1955. Contains "This
Unimportant Morning."

21d *SEVEN CENTURIES OF POETRY: CHAUCER TO
DYLAN THOMAS.* Edited by A. N. Jeffares.
London: Longmans, Green, 1955. Contains
"Swans."

22 *NEW POEMS 1956: A P.E.N. ANTHOLOGY.*
Edited by Stephen Spender, Elizabeth
Jennings, and Dannie Abse. London:
Michael Joseph, 1956. Contains "The
Octagon Room, National Gallery, '55."

22a *THE CHATTO BOOK OF MODERN POETRY, 1915-
1955.* Edited by C. Day Lewis and John
Lehmann. London: Chatto & Windus, 1956.
Contains "To Ping-Kû, Asleep;" "Nemea"
and "In the Garden: Villa Cleobolus."

22b *POETRY NOW: AN ANTHOLOGY.* Edited by
G. S. Fraser. London: Faber & Faber,
1956. Contains "A Ballad of the Good
Lord Nelson" and "Alexandria."

23 *POETIC HERITAGE: A SUNDAY TIMES
ANTHOLOGY.* Edited by John Press. London:
André Deutsch, 1957. Contains "Lesbos."

23a *THE SILVER TREASURY OF LIGHT VERSE.*
Edited by Oscar Williams. New York: New
American Library, 1957. Paperback.
Contains "A Ballad of the Good Lord
Nelson."

24 *HOMMAGE A ROY CAMPBELL.* Edited by F.-J.
Temple. Montpellier: [n.p.], 1958 [i.e.,
1959]. Illustrated. Wrappers. Contains
two contributions by Durrell. Other
contributors include F.-J. Temple, Edith
Sitwell, Richard Aldington, and Wyndham
Lewis.

25   *THE GUINNESS BOOK OF POETRY: 1956-7.*
        London: Putnam, 1958. Contains "The
        Meeting."

25a   *THE BATSFORD BOOK OF CHILDREN'S VERSE.*
        Edited by Elizabeth Jennings. London:
        Batsford, 1958. Contains "Echo."

25b   *MODERN VERSE IN ENGLISH.* Edited by David
        Cecil and Allen Tate. London: Eyre &
        Spottiswoode, 1958. Contains "Alexandria"
        and "This Unimportant Morning."

        ---. New York: Macmillan, 1958.

26   *DYLAN THOMAS, THE LEGEND AND THE POET:*
        A COLLECTION OF BIOGRAPHICAL AND CRITICAL
        ESSAYS. Edited by E. W. Tedlock. London:
        Heinemann, 1960. Contains a personal
        tribute to Thomas.

27   Clausen, Rosemarie. *THEATER: GUSTAF*
        GRUNDGENS INSZENIERT. Hamburg: Christian
        Wegner, 1960. Contains numerous
        photographs taken during the production
        of *Sappho* at Hamburg, with a brief note
        in German by Durrell. [Oblong 4to.]

27a   *ESSAYS OF OUR TIME.* Edited by Leo
        Hamalian and Edmond L. Volpe. New York:
        McGraw-Hill, 1960. Contains "La Valise,"
        an Antrobus story.

27b   *FATHER'S BEDSIDE BOOK: AN ANTHOLOGY.*
        Edited by Eric Duthie. London: Heinemann,
        1960. Contains "Case History."

27c   *THE GREAT TRAVELERS: A COLLECTION OF*
        FIRSTHAND NARRATIVES OF WAYFARERS,
        WANDERERS AND EXPLORERS IN ALL PARTS OF
        THE WORLD FROM 450 B.C. TO THE PRESENT.
        Edited with introductions by Milton

Rugoff. New York: Simon and Schuster, 1960. Contains "Wine-Shop on Cyprus" from *Bitter Lemons*.

28 *THE GUINNESS BOOK OF POETRY: 1959-1960.* London: Putnam, 1961. Contains "Cavafy."

28a *AN ANTHOLOGY OF MODERN VERSE, 1940-1969.* Edited by Elizabeth Jennings. London: Methuen, 1961. Contains "On First Looking into Loeb's Horace;" "A Prospect of Children;" "Alexandria" and "Lesbos: Song from a Play."

29 *THE WRITER'S DILEMMA: ESSAYS FIRST PUBLISHED IN THE TIMES LITERARY SUPPLEMENT.* Introduction by Stephen Spender. Oxford: Oxford University Press, 1961. Contains "No Clue to Living."

30 *PENGUIN MODERN POETS, No. 1: LAWRENCE DURRELL, ELIZABETH JENNINGS, AND R. S. THOMAS.* Harmondsworth, Middlesex: Penguin Books, 1962. Wrappers.

30a *DIONYSUS: A CASE OF VINTAGE TALES ABOUT WINE.* Collected and edited with an introduction by Clifton Fadiman. New York: McGraw-Hill, 1962. Contains "Stiff Upper Lip," an Antrobus story.

31 *INTERNATIONAL WRITERS CONFERENCE.* Edinburgh: August 1962. Contains brief note on and portrait of Durrell. [A transcript of the "Programme & Notes" of the Conference, roneoed on foolscap sheets, unbound and held in place by an office paper-holder threaded through a punched hole in left-hand top corner. Each day's proceedings numbered separately: 20 Aug. (1)-23; 21 Aug. (1)-28; 22 Aug. (1)-25; 23 Aug. (1)-27; 24 Aug. (1)-35.]

31a *MODERN BRITISH POETRY.* Edited by Louis Untermeyer. 7th revised edition. New York: Harcourt, Brace, 1962. Contains "In Arcadia;" "Swans;" "Visitations" from "Eight Aspects of Melissa," and "A Water-Colour of Venice."

32 *KAREN, BARONESS BLIXEN.* "Redigeret af Clara Svendsen og Ole Wivel." Copenhagen: Gyldenal, 1962. Portrait. Contains tribute in Danish by Durrell, reprinted from *Nordisk Verlag.*

---. *Baroness Blixen, Isak Dinesen: A Memorial.* Edited by Clara Svendsen. New York: Random House, 1965.

32a *HANS REICHEL: 1892-1958.* Paris: Editions Jeanne Bucher, 1962. Illustrated. Contains a tribute to Reichel in English, also translated into French and German.

32b Hintermeier, Maria, and Fritz Joachim Raddatz. *ROWOHLT ALMANACH 1908-1962.* Hamburg: Rowohlt, 1962. Paperback. Contains a selection from *Justine.*

32c *THE 7TH ANNUAL OF THE YEAR'S BEST S-F.* Edited by Judith Merril. New York: Simon and Schuster, 1962. Contains "High Barbary," an Antrobus story.

33 *WALTER SMART BY SOME OF HIS FRIENDS.* [Edited by Robin Fedden.] Chichester: Privately printed by Lady Smart [n.d. 1963]. Contains "Thinking about 'Smartie.'" [Limited to 500 copies.]

34 *HENRY MILLER AND THE CRITICS.* Edited by George Wickes. Carbondale: Southern Illinois University Press, 1963. Contains "Studies in Genius: Henry Miller" [See Section E: *Horizon*, XX: 115 (July 1949).]

34a   *ANTHOLOGY OF MODERN POETRY. HUTCHINSON
      ENGLISH TEXTS.* Edited by John Wain.
      London: Hutchinson, 1963. Contains
      "Dmitri of Carpathos" from "Eternal
      Contemporaries: Six Portraits;"
      "Epitaph;" "Green Man;" "Nemea" and "To
      Ping-Kû, Asleep."

34b   *DYLAN THOMAS'S CHOICE: AN ANTHOLOGY OF
      VERSE SPOKEN BY DYLAN THOMAS.* Edited by
      Ralph Maud and Aneirin Talfan Davies.
      Norfolk, Conn.: New Directions, 1963.
      Contains "Mythology."

34c   *EROTIC POETRY: THE LYRICS, BALLADS,
      IDYLLS, AND EPICS OF LOVE--CLASSICAL TO
      CONTEMPORARY.* Edited by William Cole.
      New York: Random House, 1963. Contains
      "The Adepts" from "Eight Aspects of
      Melissa," and "A Ballad of the Good Lord
      Nelson."

35   *NEW POEMS 1963: A P.E.N. ANTHOLOGY OF
      CONTEMPORARY POETRY.* Edited by Lawrence
      Durrell. London: Hutchinson, 1963. [A
      somewhat uncomplimentary review in *The
      Times Literary Supplement* brought forth
      a blistering letter from Edith Sitwell:
      "Sir,--Mr. Lawrence Durrell, who is the
      editor of the new P.E.N. Anthology, is
      in trouble with the reviewer of that
      book because he is a fine writer, and
      therefore famous. I do not know from
      under what dull, meaningless stone the
      writer of that review crawled! But I
      understand that persons of that kind
      think I am laughing at them. (They are
      all exactly alike.) There is nothing to
      be said against them as writers (apart
      from the fact that a pathological hatred
      and malice are unattractive) except for
      three things: *A* that they have nothing

whatsoever in their heads. *B* that they do not know one word from another. *C* that they can't write. Etc., etc." (5 December 1963).]

36 *THE VAMPIRE: ALL THE BEST VAMPIRE STORIES IN THE WORLD.* Presented by Roger Vandin. London: Pan Books, 1963. Paperback. Contains "Carnival" from *Balthazar*.

37 *PERMANENCES MEDITERRANEENNES DE L'HUMANISME.* Paris: Societé d'Editions Les Belles Lettres, 1963. Contains English text and translation of "Langue d'Oc," translated by F.-J. Temple. [First published in the *Revue Atlantique*, daily newspaper of the liner "France" (3 Fevrier 1962).]

37a *THE GOLDEN TREASURY OF THE BEST SONGS AND LYRICAL POEMS IN THE ENGLISH LANGUAGE.* Compiled by Francis Turner Palgrave, with a fifth book selected by John Press. London and New York: Oxford University Press, 1964. Contains "Sarajevo."

37b *OPINIONS AND PERSPECTIVES: FROM THE NEW YORK TIMES BOOK REVIEW.* Edited and with an Introduction by Francis Brown. Boston, Mass.: Houghton Mifflin, 1964. Contains "Landscape with Literary Figures."

37c *THE PURSUIT OF GREECE: AN ANTHOLOGY.* Edited by Philip Sherrard. London: John Murray, 1964. Contains "Nemea;" "Delos;" and the opening paragraph from *Prospero's Cell*.

37d *TODAY'S POETS: AMERICAN AND BRITISH*

POETRY SINCE THE 1930s. Edited by Chad Walsh. New York: Scribner, 1964. Contains "Alexandria;" "Conon in Exile;" "The Critics;" "The Lost Cities;" "On First Looking into Loeb's Horace" and "Song for Zarathustra."

38 *RICHARD ALDINGTON: AN INTIMATE PORTRAIT.* Edited by Alister Kershaw and F.-J. Temple. Carbondale: Southern Illinois University Press, 1965. Contains a short memoir by Durrell.

38a *COLLECTION GENIES ET REALITES: SHAKESPEARE.* Paris: Librairie Hachette [1962; i.e., 12 April 1965]. Contains the French translation of "Shakespeare and Love," a UNESCO address given by Durrell.

38b *MEMORABLE POETRY.* Edited by Francis Meynell. New York: Franklin Watts, 1965. Contains "Carol on Corfu."

38c *THE MID CENTURY: ENGLISH POETRY 1940-1960.* Edited by David Wright. Harmondsworth, Middlesex: Penguin Books, 1965. Contains "On First Looking into Loeb's Horace."

38d *THE OLYMPIA READER: SELECTIONS FROM THE TRAVELLER'S COMPANION SERIES.* Edited by Maurice Girodias. New York: Grove Press, 1965. Contains "The Black Book."

---. New York: Ballantine Books, 1967.

39 *THE POETRY OF RAILWAYS.* Edited by Kenneth Hopkins. London: Leslie Frewin, 1966. Contains "Night Express."

40 *I BURN FOR ENGLAND: AN ANTHOLOGY OF*

POETRY OF WORLD WAR II. Selected and introduced by Charles Hamblett. Contains "Epitaph" and "In a Time of Crisis."

41   *LONDON MAGAZINE POEMS, 1961-1966*. Selected by Hugo Williams; introduced by Alan Ross. London: Alan Ross, 1966. Contains "Leeches;" "Geishas;" "Io" and "Troy."

41a   *THE BEST OF OLYMPIA: AN ANTHOLOGY OF TALES, POEMS, SCIENTIFIC DOCUMENTS AND TRICKS WHICH APPEARED IN THE SHORT-LIVED AND MUCH LAMENTED OLYMPIA MAGAZINE. THE OLYMPIA PRESS TRAVELLER'S COMPANION SERIES*. Edited by Maurice Girodias. London: New English Library, 1966. Contains "Pursewarden's Incorrigibilia" and "Frankie and Johnny--New Style."

41b   *SOLO: AN ANTHOLOGY*. Edited by John Bayliss. London: Hamish Hamilton, 1966. Contains "Buying a House in Cyprus."

42   *L'HERNE* (Paris; 1967[?]). Contains private letter on Wyndham Lewis to Lacordaire, Lewis's translator.

42a   *ABROAD: A BOOK OF TRAVELS*. Edited by Jon Evans. London: Victor Gollancz, 1968. Contains "Delos;" "Fishing at Corfu" [an excerpt from *Prospero's Cell*], and the statement "Somewhere between Calabria and Corfu the blue really begins," also from *Prospero's Cell*.

42b   *THE BOOSTER, SEPTEMBER 1937-EASTER 1939*. New York: Johnson Reprint Corporation, 1968. [A reprint of all the issues of *The Booster* and *Delta* edited by Alfred Perlès and friends.]

42c   *POETRY OF THE FORTIES*. Edited by Robin
      Skelton. Harmondsworth, Middlesex:
      Penguin Books, 1968. Contains "This
      Unimportant Morning" and "Phileremo."

43   *THE NEW YORKER BOOK OF POEMS*. New York:
      Morrow, 1969. Contains "Paphos;"
      "Salamis" and "Stoic."

43a   *O MUNDO DE HENRY MILLER*. Edited by
      Hermenegildo Sá Cavalcante. Rio de
      Janeiro: Grafica Record Editora, 1969.
      Contains "Sexus in Discussion" and "The
      Breath of the Dragon," both in Portugese.

43b   *TO PLAY MAN NUMBER ONE*. Compiled by
      Sara Hannum and John Terry Chase. New
      York: Atheneum, 1969. Contains "Water
      Music."

43c   *BRITISH POETRY SINCE 1945*. Edited by
      Edward Lucie-Smith. Harmondsworth,
      Middlesex: Penguin Books, 1970. Contains
      "A Portrait of Theodora;" "Sarajevo" and
      "Bitter Lemons."

43d   *VOICES OF POETRY*. Edited by Allen
      Kirscher. New York: Dell, 1970.
      Paperback. Contains "Bitter Lemons."

44   *10 POETS 10 POEMS*. Collected by O. G.
      Bradbury. London: Ealing School of Art,
      1971. Contains "Last Heard Of." [Limited
      to 100 copies.]

44a   *THE PENGUIN BOOK OF MODERN QUOTATIONS*.
      Edited by J. M. and M. J. Cohen.
      Harmondsworth, Middlesex: Penguin Books,
      1971. Contains eight quotations from
      "Mythology," *Balthazar*, *Esprit de Corps*
      and *Tunc*, and one "Reported Remark:"
      "A poem is what happens when an anxiety
      meets a technique."

44b   Milligan, Spike. *MILLIGAN'S ARK*.
       Walton-on-Thames, Surrey: M. & J. Hobbs,
       1971. Contains "Study of a French Tit
       resting upon Its Laurels," a drawing by
       Oscar Epfs [Lawrence Durrell].

45   *A FESTSCHRIFT FOR DJUNA BARNES ON HER
       80TH BIRTHDAY*. [Kent, Ohio]: Kent State
       University Libraries, 1972. Contains a
       brief tribute.

45a   *FESTSCHRIFT FOR KATHERINE FALLEY BENNETT*.
       Edited by Tambimuttu. London: The Lyre
       Press, 1972. Contains "Vaumort" and
       "Draft of a Poem for K.F.B.'s Birthday."

45b   *THE LUCIFER SOCIETY: MACABRE TALES BY
       GREAT MODERN WRITERS*. Edited by Peter
       Haining, with a Foreword by Kingsley
       Amis. London: W. H. Allen & Co., Ltd.,
       1972. Contains "The Cherries." [See
       Section D.1.]

       ---. New York: Taplinger, 1972.

       ---. *Detours Into the Macabre*.
       London: Pan Books, 1974. Paperback.

45c   *CONTEMPORARY DRAMATISTS*. Edited by
       James Vinson, with a Preface by Ruby
       Cohn. London: St. James Press, 1973.
       Contains a short statement by Durrell.

       ---. New York: St. Martin, 1973.

45d   *THE OXFORD BOOK OF TWENTIETH-CENTURY
       ENGLISH VERSE*. Edited by Philip Larkin.
       London: Oxford University Press, 1973.
       Contains "Mythology;" "Poggio" and "This
       Unimportant Morning."

46   *A BOOK OF LOVE POETRY*. Edited by Jon

Stallworthy. New York: Oxford University Press, 1974. Contains "This Unimportant Morning."

47 *A CASEBOOK ON ANAIS NIN*. Edited by Robert Zaller. New York: New American Library, 1974. Contains Durrell's preface to Nin's *Children of the Albatross* (1959). [See Section C.2.] [The "Contributors" notes tell us that Durrell's "most recent book is *Pope Joan*"!]

48 *THE FABER BOOK OF COMIC VERSE*. Edited by Michael Roberts and Janet Adam Smith. Revised edition. London: Faber & Faber, 1974. Contains "Ballad of the Oedipus Complex;" "Coptic Poem" and "Epitaph."

49 *THE ROSES RACE AROUND HER NAME: POEMS FROM FATHERS TO DAUGHTERS*. Edited by Jonathan Cott. New York: Stonehill, 1974.

50 *STEAM PRESS PORTFOLIO, NO. 2*. London: The Turret Bookshop, 1974. Illustrated by Ralph Steadman. Contains "The Grey Penitents." ["Edition limited to 50 copies only numbered and signed by the authors and artist."]

51 *A CLUTCH OF VAMPIRES*. Edited by Raymond T. McNally. New York: Warner Books, 1975. Contains "Vampire in Venice," Pursewarden's story from *Balthazar*.

52 *CONTEMPORARY POETS*. Edited by James Vinson, with a Preface by C. Day Lewis. 2nd edition. London: St. James Press, 1975. Contains a short statement by Durrell.

---. New York: St. Martin, 1975.

53   *GEORGE SEFERIS 1900-1971: CATALOGUE OF
      AN EXHIBITION ARRANGED BY THE NATIONAL
      BOOK LEAGUE AND THE BRITISH COUNCIL.*
      London: Greek Month (5 November-
      5 December) 1975. Contains "On George
      Seferis."

54   Skelton, Robin. *THE POET'S CALLING.*
      London: Heinemann, 1975. Contains a
      quotation from *The Red Limbo Lingo.*

      ---. New York: Barnes & Noble, 1975.

55   Izis. *PARIS DES POETES.* Paris: Editions
      Fernand Nathan, 1977. Contains the
      following note: "In France, that great
      garden of cuckolds, the Socratic questions
      are still asked even though everyone is
      well aware that there are no ready answers.
      The basic questions of science, love,
      husbandry and art are always there, always
      intractable, always provoking. But the
      answer is the same always--the question
      stays open like a flick-knife and the
      poor questioner is forced to be content
      with 'Ah, my friend, that remains to be
      seen.'"

56   *THE CAPRA CHAPBOOK ANTHOLOGY.* Santa
      Barbara, Calif.: Capra Press, 1979.
      Contains "The Plant-Magic Man." [See
      Section A.51b.]

57   *POETS.* Edited by Anthony Astbury and G.
      H. Godbert. London: The Greville Press,
      1979. Contains poems by Durrell, Empson,
      Graves, Spender, and others.

58   Gunton, Sharon R., and Laurie Lanzen
      Harris, *CONTEMPORARY LITERARY CRITICISM,
      XV.* Detroit: Gale Research, 1980.
      Contains a slightly shortened version of

the tribute to Odysseus Elytis which
originally appeared in *Books Abroad*
(Autumn 1975). [See Section E.]

59 *MOUNTS OF VENUS: THE PICADOR BOOK OF
EROTIC PROSE*. Edited by Alan Bold.
London: Pan Books, 1980. Paperback.
Contains a selection from *The Black Book*.

E. CONTRIBUTIONS TO PERIODICALS

ADAM: INTERNATIONAL REVIEW, Nos. 385-390.
(1974-75). Contains "Style and
Generosity," a reminiscence about Cyril
Connolly.

ALEF (Tunis) (1972). Contains "A Small Tribute
to Seferis."

ANTAEUS, No. 1 (1970). Contains a poem by
Durrell.

THE ANTIQUARIAN BOOKMAN (New York) (May-June
1962). Contains an essay on book
collecting. [See Section A.36.]

L'ARC: CAHIERS MEDITERRANEENS (Aix-en-Provence),
3e année, No. 11 (Juillet 1960). Contains
"Les citrons amers."

---.   4e année, No. 15 (Juillet 1960). Contains
"Le Becfigue," translated by F.-J. Temple.

ARGOSY (London) (January 1958). Contains "The
Ghost Train," an Antrobus story.
Illustrated by Roy Berry.

---.   (April 1963). Contains "Stiff Upper Lip,"
an Antrobus story.

---.   (August 1964). Contains "The Loneliest

Beach," an extract of two paragraphs from
Prospero's Cell.

---. (August 1966). Contains "Aunt Norah," an
Antrobus story.

THE ARYAN PATH, X: 12 (December 1939). Contains
"Tao and Its Glozes." [Reprinted in *A
Smile in the Mind's Eye* (1980); see
Section A.58.]

THE ATLANTIC (Boston) (September 1957).
Contains "Liberation Celebration Machine,"
an Antrobus story.

---. CCXV: 5 (May 1965). Contains "The Other
T. S. Eliot." [This tribute had
previously appeared in French in *Preuves*
(Paris) (April 1965).]

BANANAS: THE LITERARY MAGAZINE (London), No. 23
(October 1980). Contains "The Unseen
Poems," a selection from *Collected Poems
1931-1974* (1980) consisting of "The
Beginning;" "Dark Grecian;" "Candle-
Light;" "Echoes I;" "Echoes II;"
"Futility" and "Finis." Also contains
an early and a late photograph of
Durrell.

BOOK COLLECTING AND LIBRARY MONTHLY (Brighton),
No. 16 (August 1969). Contains "Faces
(1934)." [This poem, which Durrell
intended to include in a *festschrift*
(unpublished) for John Gawsworth's
fiftieth birthday, originally appeared
in *Transition: Poems* (1934); see
Section A.4.]

BOOKS ABROAD, XLIX (Autumn 1975). Contains
"The Poetry of Elytis."

THE BOOSTER (Paris), II: 7 (September 1937);
II: 8 (October 1937); 3e année, No. 9
(November 1937); 4e année, Nos. 10-11
(December 1937-January 1938); *Delta*,
2e année, No. 2 (April 1938); 2e année,
No. 3 (Christmas 1938); 3e année, No. 1
(Easter 1939). [A monthly in French and
English, edited by Alfred Perlès, Lawrence
Durrell, Henry Miller, and William
Saroyan. It was the magazine of the
American Country Club, who handed its
direction to Alfred Perlès in the mistaken
belief that his brilliant friends would
turn it into a sort of *New Yorker*. As
far as we know, their opinion of the
result has not been recorded. For the
history of *The Booster* and its successor,
Delta, see Perlès, *My Friend Henry Miller*
(London: Neville Spearman, 1955; New York:
John Day, 1956).

Contains numerous contributions by
Durrell and Charles Norden. Also the
first appearance in print of Gerald
Durrell, then aged eleven. Durrell
thought that Gerald's tutor, Patrick
Evans, had written the piece. "Do you
suppose," said Evans, "that if I could
write as well as that I would waste my
time on being a tutor?" The back page
usually carried a poem in some exotic
script--Persian, Japanese, and others--
produced by means of a line block.
Meanwhile the stolid bourgeois
advertisements continued to appear,
flanked by *The House of Incest* and
Nightwood.]

BOSTON UNIVERSITY JOURNAL, XXIII: 2 (1975).
Contains "The Mysteries of Tutankhamen."
Illustrated. Includes "Notes to
Illustrations" by Ed Brovarski, Museum of
Fine Arts, Boston.

BULLETIN OF THE JOHN RYLANDS LIBRARY
(Manchester), XXVII: 1 (Winter 1942).
Contains George Seferis, "Myth of Our
History," translated by Durrell and G.
Katsimbalis.

CHIMERA (New York), III: 3 (Spring 1945).
Contains "Byron."

---, V: 2 (Winter 1947). Contains "Eternal
Contemporaries."

CIRCLE NINE (Berkeley, Calif.) (1946). Contains
"Eight Aspects of Melissa." [The magazine
appeared in four different covers, all
executed by Bezadel Schatz.]

COUNTERPOINT, I: 1 (n.d. [1945-46]). Contains
"Conon the Critic on the Six Landscape
Painters of Greece."

THE CRITIC (Chicago) (December 1966-January
1967). Contains "Seraglios and
Imbroglios," an Antrobus story.

CYPRUS REVIEW, X: 10 (October 1954). Contains
"Beccafico: a tragic history." With ten
photographs. Unsigned. [An early form
of the limited edition published by La
Licorne in January 1963; see Section A.
38.
    This issue of the *Review* was supposed
to have been the first edited by Durrell,
who continued as editor until the end
of 1955 (see Section H., Potter and
Whiting [1961], Item 158). However, an
editorial note in the September 1955
number bids farewell to George Curwen
Wilkinson as editor, thus bringing into
question Durrell's editorial involvement.]

---. XI: 4 (April 1955). Contains "G. Pol

Georghiou," a discussion of the work of
the Cypriot painter, with color plates.
Signed "L. D."

---. XI: 7 (July 1955). Contains "Plus ça
change: A Mental Excavation." Terracotta
figures from the Cyprus Museum with
contemporary comments.

THE DAILY EXPRESS (London) (8 December 1964).
Contains an article, "Claude Seignolle."

THE DAILY MAIL (London) (22 August 1974).
Contains "This Magnetic, Bedevilled
Island that Tugs at My Heart."

THE DAILY TELEGRAPH MAGAZINE (London), No. 452
(29 June 1973). Contains "The Plant-
Magic Man." Illustrated.

DAYLIGHT (London), I (1941). Contains five
poems by George Seferis, translated by
Durrell and G. Katsimbalis.

DELTA (Paris), 2e année, No. 2 (April 1938).
Contains "Poem to Gerald." [A
continuation of *The Booster* with the
same editors.]

---. 2e année, No. 3 (Christmas 1938).
Contains "Hamlet Prince of China." [The
January 1937 letter which was the original
of this article was included in the
Private Correspondence (1963) by George
Wickes, who noted that "minor changes"
were made to the original before
publication. Of 247 lines of type in
the *Delta* article, 80 do not appear in
Wickes's edition of the correspondence.
In other words, one-third of the *Delta*
article consisted of what Wickes calls
"minor changes."]

---. 2^eannée, No. 4 (Easter 1939). Contains "The Sonnet of Hamlet." [This number was published in London.]

DIOGENES (Madison, Wis.), I: 3 (Autumn 1941). Contains "Letter to Seferis the Greek."

DIRE (Montpellier), Nos. 4-5 (Printemps-Eté 1963). Contains "Piccadilly" and "Ode to a Lukewarm Eyebrow." Translated by F.-J. Temple. Linocuts by Bessil. ["Mr. Durrell and Miss Compton Burnett meet with such praise in France as to raise many a lukewarm English eyebrow. . . . There is something in the English temper that loves a shortage, be it of words. . ." (*Times Literary Supplement*).]

---. 6 (Automne 1963). Contains "Un Faust Irlandais (Scène Huit)." Translated by F.-J. Temple.

THE ECONOMIST (London) (24 July 1954). Contains "The Cypriot's Dilemma."

---. (13 August 1954). Contains "Hush Over Cyprus."

---. (29 October 1954). Contains "Cypriots Watch and Wait."

---. (24 September 1955). Contains "Hellenism in Danger."

["Mr. Durrell made other contributions to *The Economist* in 1954 and 1955 but chiefly in the form of letters which were then used as a basis for editorials written in London."]

EGYPTIAN GAZETTE (Cairo) (April-December 1941). Numerous contributions by Durrell. *"Some time between April 1941 and the end of*

*that year I ran a weekly funny column in
the Egyptian Gazette. Pure rubbish in
the Beachcomber vein. It earned me about
ten pounds a month which as a refugee I
needed. I didn't get taken on at the
Embassy until August of that year I
think. Me and Rimbaud both! Searchers
might look out for Aunt Norah who
featured in this column. I also wrote
numberless leaders (perhaps 15) on policy
matters then deemed important. One,
called "Quo Vadis?", got a spate of
telephone calls and fan letters. Why?
It is a mystery. It was a stupendously
banal piece--but on the party line!"*

ELLE (Paris), No. 1046 (Janvier 1966 *et seq.*).
    Contains "Judith, le nouveau roman de
    Lawrence Durrell."

ENCOUNTER (London), IX (December 1957).
    Contains "The Shades of Dylan Thomas."

---. XVIII (September 1961). Contains
    "Aphrodite" and "A Persian Lady."

---. XXI (October 1963). Contains "Byzance."

---. XXVIII (January 1967). Contains "Blood-
    Count."

---. XXVIII (March 1967). Contains "Moonlight."

---. XXXVII (August 1971). Contains "Ophite."

---. XLIII (October 1974). Contains "Patch
    of Dust."

ENVOY (June 1967). Contains "Press Interview."

ESQUIRE (Chicago), LIII: 2 (February 1960).
    Contains "Clea." [The first publication

in America of a significant portion of
Clea.]

THE EVENING STANDARD (London) (22 November
1957). Contains "Letter in the Sofa" in
the *Did It Happen?* series. Reprinted in
The Glasgow Evening Citizen (17 January
1959).

---. (8 February 1958). Contains "The
Disquieting American." Reprinted in *The
Evening Chronicle* (Manchester) (12 May
1958); *The Glasgow Evening Citizen*
(15 October 1959); and as "The Disquieting
Yank" in *The Hunts Post* (13 June 1963).

EXPERIMENTAL REVIEW (Woodstock, N.Y.), No. 2
(November 1940). Contains "The Sermon."

---. No. 3 (September 1941). Contains
"Hanged Man;" "Three Carols;" "In Crisis;"
"Father Nicholas;" "Sermon of One;"
"Three Sons" and "Fangbrand." [These
poems were from the manuscript of *A
Private Country*, then unpublished.]

FENIX (Montpellier), No. 1 (January 1966).
Contains "Prix Blondel, A Poem,"
translated into French by F.-J. Temple.

FRANKFURTER ALLGEMEINE ZEITUNG (Frankfurt)
(8 December 1967). Contains "Der
unmögliche Attaché," from the collection
Esprit de Corps which was published the
following year. [See Section A.44a.]

FURIOSO (New Haven, Conn.), I: 4 (Summer 1941).
Contains "Carol in Corfu" and "In
Arcadia."

GANGREL (London) (n.d. [January 1945 or after]).

Contains "Conon in Alexandria."

GAZEBO (Bath) (June 1963). Contains "A Modern
    Troubadour." Illustrated by V. Webb.
    [Edited and published at Kingswood School
    as a contribution to the Freedom from
    Hunger Campaign.]

GENTLEMEN'S QUARTERLY (New York), XXVIII: 5
    (September 1959). Contains "The Iron
    Hand," an Antrobus story.

GEOGRAPHICAL MAGAZINE (London), VIII: 5 (March
    1939). Contains "Corfu: Isle of Legend."
    Illustrated. [Photographs by Nancy
    Durrell.]

---. XX: 6 (October 1947). Contains "The
    Island of the Rose," an article about
    Rhodes "by Laurence Durrell." Illustrated.
    [Photographs by the author.]

GETAWAY: CANADA'S TRAVEL MAGAZINE, IV: 1 (1980).
    Contains "Mykonos the Unsullied," an
    excerpt from *The Greek Islands*. [See
    Section A.56.] Illustrated.

GREEK HERITAGE (Athens) (Winter 1963). Edited
    by Kimon Friar. Contains "Grecian Olives"
    and "Scaffoldings: Plaka."

GREEK HORIZONS (Athens), I: 1 (Summer 1946).
    Contains "The Telephone." ["In 1946 I
    was living in Athens, and as there were a
    number of gifted young English writers all
    working in Greece, I decided that it would
    be interesting to produce a literary
    quarterly called Greek Horizons. All my
    writer friends welcomed the idea, and
    Lawrence Durrell, who was then working as
    a British Information Officer, gave me a
    short story, The Telephone. Other

contributors were Patrick Leigh Fermor,
Osbert Lancaster, Steven Runciman, John
Waller, and myself" (note by Derek
Patmore).]

GRIEVE (Charleville, France) [n.d.] Contains a
Note on the poetry of Marc Alyn.

HARPER'S BAZAAR (London), XCV (January 1962).
Contains "High Barbary," an Antrobus story.

---. CII: 3085 (December 1969). Contains
"Brassaï." Illustrated.

---. CIII: 3106 (September 1970). Contains
"Rain, Rain, go to Spain."

HARPER'S MAGAZINE, CCXXXVIII: 1426 (March 1969).
Contains "Sixties."

HOLIDAY (Philadelphia), XXV: 1 (January 1959).
Contains "The Worldly University of
Grenoble."

---. XXVI: 5 (November 1959). Contains "Ripe
Living in Provence."

---. XXVII: 1 (January 1960). Contains "Rhône."

---. XXIX: 1 (January 1961). Contains "Geneva."

---. XXIX: 2 (February 1961). Contains "Laura:
A Portrait of Avignon."

---. XXX: 8 (August 1962). Contains "Postman's
Palace--In Praise of Fanatics."

---. XXXIII: 1 (January 1963). Contains "The
Gascon Touch."

---. XXXIII: 4 (April 1963). Contains "Lawrence
Durrell Replies," a response to a letter

from George C. Maloney concerning "Gascon
Touch."

---. XL: 10 (October 1966). Contains "Oil for
the Saint," a piece about a return to
Koloura in Corfu.

---. XLIV: 2 (August 1968). Contains "Owed to
America."

---. XLV: 4 (April 1969). Contains "Justine:
Behind the Novels and the Motion Picture."
Illustrated. [The illustrations are
photographs of Alexandria by John Bulmer
and stills from the motion picture.]

HORIZON (London), XVII: 102 (June 1948). Contains
"Studies in Genius VI: Groddeck."

---. XX: 115 (July 1949). Contains "Studies in
Genius VIII: Henry Miller."

INTERNATIONAL (London), I: 2 (Spring 1965).
Contains "The Most Remarkable Frenchwoman
of Our Time" [Alexandra David-Neele].
Illustrated. [Translation into French
appears in *Elle* (Paris), 17 Juillet 1964.]

INTERNATIONAL POST (London), I: 1 (6 April 1939).
Contains "Sense and Sensibility," a review
of "Heaven and Charing Cross" by A. Danvers
Walker and "Family Reunion" by T. S. Eliot.
[Durrell was appointed drama critic for
this weekly review of the arts and letters
which was edited by Christopher Rowan
Robinson and Tristram Pownall. The other
weekly contributors included Swane Fox
(Art), Cyril Beaumont (Ballet), John
Gawsworth (Books), Eric Halpenny (Music),
Edward Carrick (Cinema), and Geoffrey
Mordaunt (Television). Anthony Knerr
first recorded the existence of this item,

but, as he had seen only a paste-up and
could trace no published copies, he assumed
that it was unpublished. Other compilers
of Durrell bibliographies followed him in
that assumption. Later, in 1969, John
Gawsworth referred to the item in *Book
Collecting and Library Monthly* (Brighton),
No. 16 (August). "'In my Great James
Street days,' he said, 'any ring at the
bell might be Larry, as we were colleagues
on a small paper. I think it was called
International Post but only the first
issue was ever published.'" The paste-up
which Knerr saw appeared in Catalogue
No. 84 issued by The House of Books (New
York), but a published copy turned up in
a Brighton bookshop in May 1974.

The item is 4.9 inches by 7.3 inches,
quarto, with staple binding. Both the
inside front and back covers are printed,
but the outside back cover and leaf 11*v*
are blank. The yellow card cover (which
Gawsworth remembered) is vertically
striped in light blue on the front. The
issue was printed by Service Printing Co.,
Rear 240 Wickham Road, Shirley, Croydon.]

ISIS (Oxford), No. 1552 (21 February 1968).
Contains "The Outer Limits."

KINGDOM COME: THE MAGAZINE OF WAR-TIME OXFORD,
I: 4 (Summer 1940). Edited by John Waller
and others. Contains "In Arcadia."

KING'S SCHOOL REVIEW (Canterbury), I: 2 (March
1960). Contains "The Moonlight of Your
Smile." The editorial states: "Two weeks
ago a profile of Lawrence Durrell in *The
Observer* stated, quite incorrectly, that
he was educated at King's. On these
grounds alone we wrote asking him for a
contribution and were sent the excellent

short story featured in this issue. Also
enclosed was a letter: *'I apologize for
the nasty smear in The Observer. I wasn't
responsible and indeed haven't seen it. I
send you a short article as a form of
apology. I hope you can mention that I
was educated at St. Edmund's or they may
march on you. . . . I hope my name won't
get you birched by the head.'"*

LABRYS 5: LAWRENCE DURRELL SPECIAL ISSUE (London)
(July 1979). Contains "Constance in Love,"
an excerpt from *Constance*, volume three of
the *Avignon Quintet*; "Sappho and After;"
"Letters to Jean Fanchette," and "Lawrence
Durrell Answers a Few Questions."

LES LETTRES NOUVELLES (22 Avril 1959). Contains
"Carnaval à Alexandrie," an excerpt from
Balthazar translated into French by Roger
Giroux.

LILLIPUT (London) (March 1958). Contains "La
Valise," an Antrobus story.

THE LISTENER (London) (18 September 1947).
Contains "Greek Peasant Superstitions."

---.   (25 September 1947). Contains "Can Dreams
Live On When Dreamers Die?"

---.   (27 October 1966). Contains letter
replying to Alexander Cockburn's review
of *Sauve Qui Peut.*

---.   (20 April 1978). Contains "Alexandria
and After--Lawrence Durrell in Egypt."

LITERARISCHES ARBEITS JOURNAL (Nürnberg), No. 5
(1980). Contains "The Plant-Magic Man,"
translated into German by Manfred Vogel.
Two illustrations, and facsimile of "Le
Paradis des Plantes" catalog.

LITTACK (Epping), II: 2 (March 1974). Contains "In Deep Grass" and a letter from Durrell containing "Les Douzes Commandements," "an indispensible guide to the creation of a work of art" [which later appeared as a note in *Livia, or Buried Alive* (1978); see Section A.57].

LONDON MAGAZINE, I: 8 (September 1954). Contains "Letters in Darkness."

---. I: 9 (October 1954). Contains "Cypriot Poetry: A Little Anthology," translated by Maurice Cardiff and Lawrence Durrell.

---. III: 7 (July 1956). Contains "A Cavafy Find," three poems by C. P. Cavafy translated by Durrell.

---. IV: 4 (April 1957). Contains review of books by Roy Fuller, D. J. Enright, and Philip Larkin.

---. IV: 7 (July 1957). Contains "How to Buy a House in Cyprus."

---. n.s. I: 11 (February 1962). Contains "Context," replies--together with other poets--to six questions on modern poetry.

---. n.s. III: 9 (December 1963). Contains "Stone Honey;" "Scaffoldings," and "Strip Tease."

---. n.s. III: 10 (January 1964). Contains "Bernard Spencer: A Memoir," preface to Spencer's *Last Poems*.

---. n.s. V: 4 (July 1965). Contains "Io;" "Troy;" "Leeches," and "Geishas."

---. n.s. VI: 12 (March 1967). Contains "Confederate."

LUI (Paris and New York) (June 1964). Contains "Lawrence du Midi" [Reflections about Women].

MADEMOISELLE (New York), XLVIII (March 1959). Contains "Tree of Extremity," an excerpt from *Mountolive*. Portrait.

---. L (February 1960). Contains "Capital of Memory."

---. LIII (September 1961). Contains "High Barbary," an Antrobus story.

---. LVI (January 1963). Contains "Lawrence Durrell and Henry Miller: A Private Correspondence," a selection from the book edited by George Wickes. [See A.37.]

---. LVII (September 1963). Contains "What Ho on the Rialto," an Antrobus story.

---. LX (November 1964). Contains "Scaffoldings;" "In the Margin," and "Poemandres."

---. LXIV (December 1966). Contains "Taking the Consequences," an Antrobus story.

THE MALAHAT REVIEW (Victoria, British Columbia), No. 27 (July 1971). Contains "A Farewell" and "Apesong."

---. XLII (April 1977). Contains "Gog and Magog, Being the First Chapter of a Novel entitled *Livia, or Buried Alive*." [This version differs slightly from that in the novel.]

MAN ABOUT TOWN (London), II: 1 (January 1961). Contains "Mr. Ought and Mrs. Should" (Anxieties of Our Time).

MERCURE DE FRANCE (Paris) (3 February 1972). Contains a note on Jules Laforgue.

MERKUR (Stuttgart) (September 1958). Contains "Zwielicht in Alexandria," a pre-publication excerpt from *Justine*.

DER MONAT (Berlin) (März 1959). Contains "Alexandria," a pre-publication excerpt from *Balthazar*.

MOSAIC--THE WORLD OF ANAIS NIN (Winnipeg, Manitoba), II: 2 (Winter 1978). Contains a photo and a personal comment (dated April 1977) on Nin's courage in providing a preface to Miller's *Tropic of Cancer*.

NATION (New York), CLXXXVII: 2 (19 July 1958). Contains "Cyprus: Personal Reflections."

NEUROTICA (U.S.A.), No. 3 (Autumn 1948). Contains "Conon on Mnemons."

THE NEW ENGLISH WEEKLY (London), X: 14 (11 January 1937). Contains "The Prince and Hamlet: A Diagnosis."

---. XII: 4 (4 November 1937). Contains correspondence from *The Booster* replying to George Orwell's attack on that magazine. [Considering the references to "a poet's world" and to heraldry, and in the light of the presence of lines 3-6 of "The Ballad of Kretschmer's Types" (first published 1960), we conclude that the letter is Durrell's work.]

---. XIV: 11 (22 December 1938). Contains "Lines to Music."

---. XIV: 16 (26 January 1939). Contains "News from Paris," a review of Miller's *Max and*

the White Phagocytes. Signed "Laurence
Durrell." [The frequent misspellings of
the Christian name in early items is simply
a result of Durrell's own signature.]

---. XIV: 21 (2 March 1939). Contains "Logos."

---. XV: 14 (20 July 1939). Contains "The Open
Way."

---. XV: 21 (7 September 1939). Contains
"Journal (to David Gascoyne)" and
"Equality," a letter "mildly" protesting
a review of Edgell Rickword and Jack
Lindsay, eds., The Handbook of Freedom
(signed "Laurence Durrell").

---. XVI: 1 (28 September 1939). Contains
"Waiting for Them" ("The Barbarians" by
Cavafy, translated by Durrell and Theodore
Stephanides).

---. XVI: 14 (25 January 1940). Contains
"Mysticism: The Yellow Peril."

---. XVI: 24 (4 April 1940). Contains "The
Underworld," a review of A. J. J.
Ratcliff, The Nature of Dreams, and R. L.
Megroz, The Dream World. Signed "L.
Durrell."

NEW HUMANIST (London), LXXXVIII: 4 (August 1972).
Contains "Seferis" and "Vega."

NEW SALTIRE (Edinburgh), No. 1 (Summer 1961).
Contains "Sappho and After."

THE NEW STATESMAN AND NATION (London), XL: 1017
(2 September 1950). Contains "Epitaph."

---. XL: 1019 (16 September 1950). Contains
"Water Colour of Venice."

---. XL: 1030 (2 December 1950). Contains "Education of a Cloud."

---. XLII: 1073 (29 September 1951). Contains "Cradle Song."

---. XLII: 1078 (3 November 1951). Contains "Chanel."

---. XLV: 1154 (18 April 1953). Contains "A Bowl of Roses."

---. L: 1282 (1 October 1955). Contains "Nicosia."

---. LI: 1304 (10 March 1956). Contains "Bitter Lemons."

---. LII: 1335 (13 October 1956). Contains "Mythology."

---. LII: 1338 (3 November 1956). Contains a review, "Travellers' Tales."

---. LII: 1344 (15 December 1956). Contains a review, "Greece Interpreted."

---. LIII: 1348 (12 January 1957). Contains "The Moulder of Minds."

---. LIII: 1360 (6 April 1957). Contains "Cry Wolf," an Antrobus story.

---. LIII: 1364 (4 May 1957). Contains a review, "Poets' Kingdoms."

---. LXXXIII: 2131 (21 January 1972). Contains "Pistol Weather."

---. LXXXVIII: 2259 (5 July 1974). Contains "Picture of Geishas."

NEW YORK HERALD TRIBUNE BOOK REVIEW (23 August

1959). Contains "His Ship Came In and
All is Well."

THE NEW YORK TIMES (23 August 1974). Contains
"Must the Lemons Remain Bitter?" A
commentary on Cyprus.

THE NEW YORK TIMES BOOK REVIEW (12 June 1960).
Contains "Landscape with Literary Figures."

---. (4 December 1960). Contains "These I've
Read and Will Read Again," answers to
questions about books he has read lately.

---. (15 January 1961). Contains "A Traveller
in Egypt," a review of E. M. Forster's
Alexandria.

---. (9 April 1972). Contains a review of
Francis Stuart's *Black List*.

---. (21 January 1973). Contains a review of
C. P. Cavafy's *Selected Poems*.

---. (19 June 1977). Contains "Selection," a
portrait of Greek poet Angelos Sekilianos
from *Sicilian Carousel*.

THE NEW YORK TIMES MAGAZINE (11 June 1978).
Contains "With Durrell in Egypt."
Illustrated. [Written in connection with
his work on the BBC2 production of "Spirit
of Place: Lawrence Durrell's Egypt."
Resulted in two letters: Conchita Ryan
Collins, 9 July 1978, and Walter A. Simon,
12 November 1978.]

THE NEW YORKER, XLI (6 November 1965). Contains
"Delphi."

---. XLI (20 November 1965). Contains
"Salamis."

---. XLII (26 March 1966). Contains "Paphos."

---. XLIV (4 January 1969). Contains "Stoic."

NIGHT AND DAY (London) (9 September 1937).
Contains "Obituary Notice: A Tragedy" by
Charles Norden, illustrated by Nancy
Norden.

LA NOUVELLE REVUE FRANCAISE, 14e année, No. 162
(1 June 1966). Contains "Blind Homer;"
"On Ithaca Standing;" "Egyptian Poem;"
"Exile in Athens;" "On Rhodes;" "A
Portrait of Theodora" and "Fabre," all
translated by Alain Bosquet.

NOVA (March 1968). Contains "Tunc," a selection
from the novel. Illustrated.

NOW (London), VIII (May–June, n.d. [post-1947]).
Contains "Elegy on the Closing of the
French Brothels."

THE OBSERVER (London) (22 October 1961).
Contains "Eleusis."

---. (28 April 1963). Contains "Congenies."

OLYMPIA (Paris), No. 1 (1962). Contains
"Pursewarden's Incorrigibilia" and
"Frankie and Johnny (New Style)."
Portrait.

ORIENTATIONS: A FORCES QUARTERLY (Cairo), I: 1
(n.d.). Edited by G. S. Fraser. Contains
"A Landscape Gone" by Charles Norden.
[Surely "A Landmark Gone"?]

PARIS REVIEW, No. 29 (Winter–Spring 1963).
Contains six of the Durrell–Miller letters.
Portrait.

PARNASSOS (Greek Cultural Society of New York),

I: 2 (Autumn 1960). Contains "To Argos,"
printed with the Greek translation of the
poem and with an illustration by Ghika.

PARTISAN REVIEW (New York), VII: 5 (n.d.).
Contains "Nemea."

---. XII: 3 (Summer 1945). Contains "In
Europe."

---. XIII: 5 (November-December 1946). Contains
"Rodini" and "Blind Homer."

PENGUIN NEW WRITING (London and New York),
No. 29 (Autumn 1946). Edited by John
Lehmann. Contains "Eternal Contemporaries"
[but only four of the six].

---. No. 32 (1947). Contains "From a Winter
Journal."

---. No. 33 (1948). Contains "The Death Feast
of the Greeks" by Angelos Sekilianos,
translated by Durrell.

THE PEOPLE (London) (2 February 1958). Contains
"Did Emily Brontë live again in Dylan?
. . . strange and mystic theory. . . put
forward by Lawrence Durrell."

PERSONAL LANDSCAPE (Cairo), No. 1 (January 1942).
A magazine of "exile" edited by Robin
Fedden, Lawrence Durrell, and Bernard
Spencer [See also Section D.11.] Contains
"To Argos;" "To Ping-Kû, Asleep;" "'Je est
un autre'" and "Ideas about Poems."

---. No. 2 (March 1942). Contains "Ideas about
Poems, 2."

---. No. 3 (June 1942). Contains "Conon in
Exile."

---. I: 4 (1942). Contains "For a Nursery Mirror" and "The Heraldic Universe."

---. II: 1 (1943). Contains "On First Looking into Loeb's Horace" and "Mythology."

---. II: 2 (1944). Contains "La Rochefoucauld" and "The Poet Reviews Himself."

---. II: 3 (1944). Contains "Byron."

---. II: 4 (1945). Contains "Conon in Alexandria."

---. Nendeln, Liechtenstein: Kraus Reprint Corporation, 1969. Photofacsimile.

[See Section H.: Robin Fedden, *Personal Landscape* (1966) for an account of this magazine.]

PLAYBOY (Chicago), X: 12 (December 1963). Contains "A Corking Evening," an Antrobus story.

---. XI: 12 (December 1964). Contains "Sauve Qui Peut," an Antrobus story.

---. XIII: 9 (September 1966). Contains "All to Scale," an Antrobus story.

---. XV: 12 (December 1968). Contains "On Creativity," an answer to the question "Do creative people have any characteristics in common, in their backgrounds or their personalities, that can be identified as wellsprings of that creativity?" Illustrated with a portrait by William Utterback.

---. XIX: 12 (December 1972). Contains "Spring Song" and "Hey, Mister, There's a Bulge in Your Computer."

POETRY (LONDON), I: 1 (February 1939). Edited
by Tambimuttu. Contains "Epitaph" and
"Island Fugue."

---. I: 2 (April 1939). Contains a letter to
Tambimuttu and a review of T. S. Eliot's
"Family Reunion."

---. I: 3 (November 1940). Contains "A
Noctuary;" "The Green Man," and a review
of Rilke's *Duino Elegies*.

---. I: 4 (January-February 1941). Contains
"In a Time of Crisis."

---. I: 5 (March-April 1941). Contains
"Daphnis and Chloë."

---. I: 6 (May-June 1941). Contains "Hero."

---. II: 7 (October-November 1942). Contains
"Epidaurus."

---. II: 10 (1944). Contains "Refugee Poets
in Africa," a letter to Tambimuttu.

---. III: 11 (September-October 1947).
Contains "In the Garden of the Villa
Cleobolus."

---. IV: 13 (June-July 1948). Contains
"Funchal;" "Teneriffe," and "Sierra."

---. IV: 14 (November-December 1948). Contains
"Self to Not-Self."

POETRY AND POVERTY (London), No. 2 (n.d.).
Contains "Clouds of Glory." [Potter and
Whiting have tentatively dated this item
as 1951 (see Section H.: Potter and
Whiting (1961), item 137). One of the
problems with this magazine is that it

appeared only "once in a way" rather than
regularly, as the second number states.
There is no date of publication given for
any of the issues.

One way of dealing with the problem is
to check publication dates of books
reviewed and/or advertised in a particular
issue. This we have done for No. 2, and,
on the basis of our findings, we conclude
that this number appeared in 1952.]

POETRY BOOK SOCIETY BULLETIN (London), No. 6
(June 1955). Contains about twenty lines
on poetry in general.

POETRY LONDON/APPLE MAGAZINE (London), I: 1
(Autumn 1979). Edited by Tambimuttu.
Contains "Apple Grammar."

POETRY LONDON-NEW YORK (New York), No. 1
(March-April 1956). Contains a letter to
Tambimuttu (dated 2 February 1954) about
a proposed book of tributes to Dylan
Thomas.

---. No. 2 (Winter 1956). Contains "At the
Long Bar."

---. No. 3 (Winter 1957). Contains "Eva Braun's
Dream."

POETRY REVIEW (London), XLI: 6 (November-
December 1950). Contains "Deus Loci."

---. XLIII: 1 (January-February 1952).
Contains "Constant Zarian, Triple Exile."

POETRY WORLD (New York), X: 12 and XI: 1 (July-
August 1939) [same issue]. Contains "The
Sonnet of Hamlet."

POST (Philadelphia) (4 June 1966). Contains

"The Little Affair in Paris," an Antrobus
story.

PREUVES (Paris), No. 170 (April 1965). Contains
"Tse-lio-t," the French translation of
the tribute to T. S. Eliot which appeared
the following month in *The Atlantic*.

PURPOSE (London), X: 3 (July-September 1938).
Contains "Egyptian Pastiche." [Later
collected as "Egyptian Poem."]

---. XI (April-June 1939). Contains "The
Simple Art of Truth: A First Study in
Doctor Graham Howe," a review of Howe's
Time and the Child.

---. XII: 2 (April-June 1940). Contains "In
Crisis," signed "Laurence Durrell."

THE QUARTERLY REVIEW OF LITERATURE, VI (1951).
Contains *Sappho*, scenes 1-3.

QUEEN (London) (31 March 1959). Contains
"Antrobus Commits a Felony" ["A Smircher
Smirched"].

RADIO TIMES (London) (8-14 April 1978).
Contains "Alexandria revisited," an
article in connection with the first
showing of "Spirit of Place: Lawrence
Durrell's Egypt" on 9 April 1978.

REALITES (Paris and New York), No. 120 (November
1960). Contains "I Wish One Could Be
More Like the Birds--to Sing Unfaltering,
at Peace."

---. No. 127 (June 1961). Contains "Women of
the Mediterranean."

---. No. 168 (November 1964). Contains

"Durrell at Delphi." [Later published in *Venture* (New York).]

---. No. 369 (November 1976). Contains "Retour à l'Egypte," an excerpt from *Monsieur, ou Le Prince des Ténèbres* (Editions Gallimard, Novembre 1976).

REPORTER, XXXIV (10 March 1966). Contains "Acropolis: 200 Drachmae" and "Apteros."

REUNION PUBLICATION TRIMESTRAL (Buenos Aires), I: 1 (Primavera de 1948). Contains "El Pensamiento de Groddeck."

RHINOZeros (Itzehoe, Germany) (1962). [An experimental typographic-calligraphic magazine.] Contains two pages reproducing Durrell's handwriting, the first in Greek and the second in English (the latter with drawings), decorated with irregular lines of type.

---. (1964). Contains one page in French and German.

RIGHT REVIEW (London) (January 1939). Contains "A Letter from the Land of the Gods."

SAMTIDEN: TIDSSKRIFT FOR POLITIKK, LITTERATUR OG SAMFUNNSSPORSMAL, LXXI: 4 (1962). Contains "Tre dikt av Lawrence Durrell," three poems translated into Norwegian by Ingvar Hauge.

SATURDAY EVENING POST (New York) (14 June 1966). Contains "The Little Affair in Paris," an Antrobus story.

---. (November 1977). Contains "Sicilian Carousel."

SATURDAY REVIEW (New York) (5 December 1964).
Contains "Portfolio."

SCENE (New York), VIII: 5 (October 1962).
Contains "Trio" ["At the Long Bar," "A
Portrait of Theodora," and "Ballad of
Psychoanalysis."]

DAS SCHOENSTE (München) (Mai 1962). Contains
"Seefahrt nach Osten," a pre-publication
excerpt from *Bitter Lemons*.

SEVEN (Taunton), No. 1 (Summer 1938). Contains
"Ego."

---.   No. 3 (Winter 1938). Contains "Asylum in
the Snow" and "Carol in Corfu."

---.   No. 4 (Spring 1939). Contains "The Ego's
Own Egg;" "The Hanged Man;" "Father
Nicholas His Death;" "The Poet, I;" "A
Small Scripture," and "Adam."

---.   No. 6 (Fall 1939). Contains "Zero."

---,   [Cambridge,] No. 7 (Christmas 1939).
Contains translations, with Stephanides
and Katsimbalis, of Seferis's "Message
in a Bottle" and "Untitled Poem."

---.   No. 8 (Spring 1940). Contains "At Nemea."

SHOW (New York) (December 1961). Contains
"Acte," with an introduction.

SOURCES (Belgium) (n.d.). Contains "Hommages"
for Alain Bosquet. [Special number.]

THE SPECTATOR (London), CXC: 6,513 (24 April
1953). Contains "Lesbos."

THE SUNDAY TELEGRAPH (London) (26 March 1961).

Contains a review of E. M. Forster's
Alexandria: A History and a Guide.

THE SUNDAY TIMES (London) (23 February 1958).
Contains "If Garlic be the Food of Love,"
an Antrobus story.

---. (9 March 1958). Contains "Antrobus and
the Bees in the Chancery."

---. (23 March 1958). Contains "The Game's
the Thing," an Antrobus story.

---. (6 April 1958). Contains "The Unspeakable
Attaché," an Antrobus story.

---. (20 April 1958). Contains "The Iron
Hand," an Antrobus story.

---. (4 May 1958). Contains "Something à la
Carte," an Antrobus story.

---. (18 May 1958). Contains "The Old
Training," an Antrobus story.

---. (9 November 1958). Contains "Experts on
Egypt," a review of J. and S. Lacouture,
Egypt in Transition.

---. (27 September 1959). Contains "The
Tassili Adventure," a review of H. Lhote,
The Search for the Tassili Frescoes.

---. (27 December 1959). Contains "The
Complete Traveller's Handbook of Hazards."

---. (3 January 1960). Contains "A Traveller's
Sorrows."

---. (22 December 1963). Contains "The
Foundation," a letter about African
dancers being provided with brassieres

when dancing before the Duke of Edinburgh.

THE SUNDAY TIMES MAGAZINE (London) (14 May 1978).
Contains "The Return of the Writer's
Friend," an article on the return of
Bernard Stone to the bookselling trade
with a new shop in Covent Garden.
Illustrated. [The illustration is a
collage of Stone by Ralph Steadman. It
was originally done as a sample for a
book of such collages which Steadman
intended to do. The book never came off,
and Stone had assumed that the sample had
been destroyed by Steadman, so he was most
surprised to see it in *The Sunday Times*.]

SYNTHESES--HENRY MILLER SPECIAL NUMBER
(Brussels), No. 249/250 (February-March
1967). Contains "Le Souffle du Dragon,"
translated by Pierre Lesdain. [Other
contributors include Anaïs Nin, Brassaï,
Alfred Perlès and F.-J. Temple.]

3 ARTS QUARTERLY, No. 2 (Summer 1960). Contains
"First Steps," on the first production
of *Sappho*.

---. No. 3 (Autumn 1960). Contains "Cavafy."

ΤΑΧΥΔΡΟΜΟΣ [*POSTMAN*] (Cairo) (15 August 1944).
Contains "Tinos in August," a poem
dedicated to Theodore Stephanides and
translated into Greek by E. Psara.

TEXAS QUARTERLY, XI: 3 (Autumn 1968). Contains
"Lake Music."

THEATRE HEUTE (Hannover) (Januar 1962). [See
Section H.: *Theater Heute* (1962).]

T'IEN HSIA MONTHLY (Shanghai), IX: 2 (September
1939). Contains "Prospero's Isle ('to

Caliban')."

TIME AND TIDE (London) (30 September 1936 or
1937).   Contains "Ionian Profile" by
Charles Norden, dedicated to Theodore
Stephanides.

———.   XXXII: 49 (8 December 1951).   Contains
"Clouds of Glory."

———.   XXXVII: 48 (1 December 1956).   Contains
"Near Paphos."

———.   XXXVII: 49 (8 December 1956).   Contains
a review of books by Kingsley Amis, John
Wain, K. Nott, W. Merwin, and Siegfried
Sassoon.

———.   XXXVIII: 11 (16 March 1957).   Contains
"Enigma Variations," a review of Pound's
Rock-Drill.

———.   XXXVIII: 16 (20 April 1957).   Contains a
review of Sergeant and Abse's *Mavericks.*

———.   XXXIX: 49 (6 December 1958).   Contains
"Old Mathieu."

THE TIMES (London) (22 May 1964).   Contains a
letter on Cyprus.

———.   (29 April 1970).   Contains "Still
Bitterness in the Lemons," an article on
Cyprus.

———.   (1 May 1971).   Contains a review of
Curtis Cate's *Life and Times of St.
Exupéry.*

THE TIMES LITERARY SUPPLEMENT (London),
No. 2,467 (13 May 1949).   Contains
"Hellene and Philhellene."   Unsigned.

---.   No. 2,556 (26 January 1951). Contains "Sarajevo."

---.   No. 2,578 (29 June 1951). Contains "The Sirens."

---.   No. 2,589 (14 September 1951). Contains "River Water."

---.   No. 2,720: Special Autumn Number (6 August 1954). Contains "On Mirrors."

---.   No. 2,813 (27 January 1956). Contains "The Octagon Room, National Gallery, '55."

---.   No. 3,039 (27 May 1960). Contains "Limits to Control III: No Clue to Living."

---.   No. 3,209 (30 August 1963). Contains a letter, "Ambiguous Gifts."

---.   No. 3,275 (3 December 1964). Contains a letter on Frank Harris.

---.   No. 3,295 (22 April 1965). Contains "Vidourle."

---.   No. 3,309 (29 July 1965). Contains "One Grey Greek Stone."

---.   No. 3,318 (30 September 1965). Contains "Prix Blondel."

---.   No. 3,345 (7 April 1966). Contains a letter, "Alexander's Tomb."

---.   No. 3,770 (7 June 1974). Contains "Certain Landfalls" and "Postmark."

---,   No. 4,039 (22 August 1980). Contains "Alexandria," a letter asking the reader's assistance in finding the

American paperback edition of E. M. Forster's *Alexandria: A History and a Guide* for which Durrell says he wrote a "very short" preface "some ten or fifteen years ago."

TOWN (London) (August 1966). Contains "The Little Affair in Paris," an Antrobus story.

TOWNSMAN (Morenstow, Cornwall), III: 12 (November 1940). Edited by Ronald Duncan. Contains "Nemea." [Originally published as "At Nemea" in *Seven* (Spring 1940), the poem was revised in the interim and this version, in both wording and format, is the first appearance of the collected poem.]

TRAVEL AND LEISURE (New York), II: 4 (Autumn 1972). Contains "The Poetic Obsession of Dublin." Illustrated.

---. III: 4 (Autumn 1973). Contains "Borromean Isles." Illustrated.

---. VI: 1 (January 1976). Contains "Sicily."

TWO CITIES (Paris), I: 3 (15 Décembre 1959). Contains a lengthy excerpt from *The Black Book* with a revised version of the "Introduction" to the Olympia Press edition.

---. I: 4 (15 Mai 1960). Contains an introduction to "Letters to Lawrence Durrell" by Dylan Thomas.

---. 7/8 (Hiver 1961). Contains "Down the Styx in an Air-Conditioned Canoe."

---. 9 (Automne 1964). Contains "Letters to

Jean Fanchette" and "Ode to a Lukewarm Eyebrow."

U. N. WORLD (New York), VI (August 1952). Contains "Family Portrait."

VENTURE (New York) (1965). Contains "Durrell at Delphi," reprinted from *Réalités*.

VIEW (New York), I (February-March 1962). Edited by Charles H. Ford and Parkes Tyler. Contains "Daphnis and Chloë."

---. III: 3 (1943). Contains "Mythology I" and "Mythology II."

VOGUE (New York and London) (April 1956). Contains "Summer."

---. (1 March 1958). Contains "A Little Game" ["Cry Wolf"], an Antrobus story.

---. (21 September 1961). Contains "The Swami's Secret," an Antrobus story.

---. (15 January 1970). Contains "One Place."

---. (May 1975). Contains "Duffy's Dublin" by "Laurence Durrell."

THE WASHINGTONIAN, XIV (February 1979). Contains "The Island that has seen Everything," an excerpt from *The Greek Islands*. Illustrated.

WEEKEND TELEGRAPH COLOUR SUPPLEMENT (London), No. 14 (23 December 1964). Contains "A Corking Evening," an Antrobus story.

---. No. 24 (5 March 1965). Contains "Sauve Qui Peut," an Antrobus story.

DIE WELT (Hamburg) (January 1960). This issue began the serialization of *Mountolive*.

THE WINDMILL (London), II: 6 (1947). Contains "From a Writer's Journal."

WOMAN'S OWN (London) (20 October 1962). Contains "Laura," a fictionalized version of an article on Avignon which originally appeared in *Holiday*.

---. (26 February-2 April 1966). Contains "Judith," serialized over five issues.

DIE ZEIT (Hamburg) (24 November 1961). Contains, with Gustaf Gründgens, "Ein Briefwechsel über das Drama Actis." Illustrated. [Slightly abridged. For the complete text, see Section A.35 and Section H.: *Theater Heute* (1962).]

---. (27 July 1962). Contains "Alle Uhren stehen Still," a short note on Rilke's novel *Die Aufzeichnungen des Malte Laurids Brigge*, translated into German by Dieter E. Zimmer.

F. RECORDINGS, MUSICAL SETTINGS,
      RADIO, TELEVISION, AND FILM
Recordings

1   *JUPITER ANTHOLOGY OF 20TH CENTURY POETRY,*
    PART II. Jupiter Recording JUR 00A2.
    Contains "Nemea," read by Pauline Letts.

2   *SONGS ABOUT GREECE.* Jupiter Recording
    JEP 0C36. Contains "Lesbos," music by
    Lennox Berkeley, and "In Arcadia," music
    by T. W. Southam, performed by Maureen
    Morelle (mezzo-soprano), Bryan Drake
    (baritone), and Diana Wright (piano).
    With a printed sheet of words. The
    picture on the sleeve is by Oscar Epfs
    [Lawrence Durrell], who used it for one
    of his Christmas cards, 1965. The
    producer wrote: "As this is not a very
    commercial recording--I doubt if we shall
    ever cover costs--Larry, with his usual
    kindness, has signed 50 numbered copies of
    the printed sheet of words."

3   *POETS READING, NO. 6: POEMS ON GREECE.*
    Jupiter Recording JEP 0C28. Contains
    "Nemea;" "To Argos;" "In Arcadia;"
    "Asphodels: Chalcidice;" "Aphrodite;"
    "Lesbos," and "Matapan." Text on sleeve
    by George Seferis.

4   *GRECIAN ECHOES: BITTER LEMONS, PROSPERO'S*
    CELL, REFLEXIONS ON A MARINE VENUS, in the
    Grands Documents de l'Histoire series.
    LVA 1003-4 (Lausanne, Switzerland).
    Selections from the "island books" chosen
    and read by Durrell.

5   *AN IRISH FAUST,* in the series *Les chefs-*

    d'oeuvre du théatre, de la littérature et
    de la poésie. . . lus par leurs auteurs.
    LVA 201 (Lausanne, Switzerland). [The
    sleeve bears facsimiles of the handwriting
    of distinguished contributors to the
    series, including Durrell.]

6   *THE LOVE POEMS OF LAWRENCE DURRELL.*
    New Rochelle, N.Y.: Spoken Arts, Inc.
    Read by Durrell at Montpellier. [The
    sleeve bears an amusing account of the
    recording session.]

7   *CONTEMPORARY POETS SET IN JAZZ.* Jupiter
    Recording JUR 0A11. Music by Wallace
    Southam, arranged by Ken Napper. Sung by
    Belle Gonzalez with jazz sextet. With a
    roneoed text. The picture on the sleeve
    is by Oscar Epfs [Lawrence Durrell], who
    used it for one of his Christmas cards,
    1965. Contains "Lesbos."

8   *SOUND OF ELEVEN: THE PETER COMTON BIG
    BAND.* 77 Records (Dobells) 77LEU12/14.
    ["*Clea* is one of three Peter Comton
    compositions on this LP which are named
    after novels by Lawrence Durrell. This
    32-bar tune is largely devoted to Mike
    Carroll's trombone playing, but Colin
    Parnell is heard in a piano solo. The
    next track *Djinn*--another Peter Comton
    original--also has a link with Lawrence
    Durrell, for the slow theme, played by
    just Ian Fenby, Ray Warleigh and bassist
    Peter Hughes, was originally entitled
    Melissa, after one of the minor characters
    in the books. . . . The concluding track
    contains two other pieces--*Mountolive* and
    Balthazar--inspired by Durrell's novels.
    Mountolive is constructed unusually, the
    eight-bar introduction being followed by
    a twelve-bar theme (not a blues), which

resolves into the opening figure. This
is succeeded by a second, and rather
similar twelve-bar tune, but with a
different chord sequence. . . . The
performance accelerates, culminating in
the percussion solo which leads into
Balthazar. This relatively conventional
32-bar tune--conventional by comparison
with *Mountolive*, anyway--has solos from
Peter Ward (on tenor sax), Ian Fenby and
Ray Warleigh" (from the sleeve by Charles
Fox).]

9   *A RECITAL OF SONGS BY ENGLISH COMPOSERS*.
    Jupiter Recording JUR 00A5. Contains
    "Nemea," music by T. W. Southam,
    performed by Wilfred Brown (tenor) and
    Margaret McNamee (piano).

10 *ULYSSES COME BACK*. London: Turret Records,
    1970. Sketch for a musical. Words and
    music by Durrell, who first plays, sings,
    and describes the work. This is then
    organized by Wallace Southam and played
    by pianist Pat Smythe with Jeff Clyne on
    the double bass, and sung by Belle
    Gonzalez. With booklet containing the
    synopsis and lyrics, numbered and signed
    by Durrell, who also painted the design
    for the record sleeve. [Limited to 99
    copies.]

Musical Settings

1   *WALKING IN MY SLEEP*. Athens: Gaetanos,
    1945. Slow foxtrot. Lyric by Larry Dell
    [Durrell], music by Tom Wallace [Wallace
    Southam].

2   *NEMEA*. London: Augener, 1950. Lyric by
    Durrell, music by T. W. Southam.

3   *AUTUMN'S LEGACY: OP. 58 FOR HIGH VOICE
     AND PIANOFORTE*, by Lennox Berkeley.
     Commissioned by the Committee of the
     Cheltenham Festival, 1962. London: J. &
     W. Chester, 1963. Contains "Lesbos."
     [First performance by Richard Lewis and
     Geoffrey Parsons.]

4   *LESBOS*. London: Oxford University Press,
     1967. Lyric by Durrell, music by T. W.
     Southam.

5   *NOTHING IS LOST, SWEET SELF*. London:
     Turret Books, 1967. Lyric by Durrell,
     music by T. W. Southam. Facsimile of
     original score. [Limited to 100 copies
     signed by author and composer.]

Radio

All references are to B.B.C. Radio. Programing
is shown according to the following set of
abbreviations:

    HS = Home Service   LP = Light Program
    TP = Third Program   Net.3 = Network Three
    R4 = Radio Four   MP = Music Program
    RL = Radio London

 9 September 1947. HS. "Greek Peasant
   Superstitions," a talk by Lawrence Durrell.

17 September 1947. HS. "China to Peru: Dreams
   and Divinations." Lawrence Durrell talks
   about ancient superstitions in modern Greece.

13 March 1948. LP. "New Books and Old Books."
   Cefalû reviewed.

19 May 1950. TP. "Poetry Now." Talk by Alan
   Ross with quotations from the poems of

Lawrence Durrell and Norman Nicholson.

15 March 1951. TP. "Lawrence Durrell: Selected Poems." Arranged and produced by Terence Tiller. [Repeated next day.]

31 July 1952. TP. "New Soundings, No.6." Edited and introduced by John Lehmann. "Deus Loci" was read. [Repeated 2 September.]

16 September 1953. HS. "The Critics." *Reflections on a Marine Venus* reviewed by Elspeth Huxley. [Repeated 17 September.]

10 July 1955. TP. "New Poetry." Introduced by Iain Fletcher. "Letters in Darkness," "Chanel," and "Sarajevo," from *The Tree of Idleness*.

28 August 1955. HS. "The Critics." *The Tree of Idleness* reviewed by G. S. Fraser. [Repeated 30 August.]

13 November 1955. HS. "The Plain Style." G. S. Fraser, the poet and critic, offers a selection of recently published poems that he has enjoyed. "Style" by Lawrence Durrell.

 4 October 1956. TP. *Freedom and Death* by Nikos Kazantzakis, reviewed by Lawrence Durrell.

 5 October 1956. TP. "The Poet's Voice: Third Programme Tenth Anniversary." An anthology of recent verse, with contributions from Lawrence Durrell.

 9 December 1956. TP. "New Poetry." Introduced by G. S. Fraser. *Selected Poems* by Lawrence Durrell.

 3 March 1957. HS. "Talking of Books." Arthur

Calder-Marshall talks about the influence of the Mediterranean scene on some contemporary writers. He refers especially to Lawrence Durrell's *Justine*.

25 March 1957. TP. *Sappho*. Adapted by Terence Tiller; incidental music by Anthony Smith-Masters. Jill Balcon in the title role.

23 April 1957. TP. "The Heraldic Universe." *Justine* reviewed by Christopher Middleton.

 4 May 1957. TP. "Recent Novels." A discussion of *Justine* by Frank Kermode, Christopher Salmon, and Angus Wilson. [Repeated 7 May.]

30 November 1957. Net.3. "The World of Books." Introduced by Robin Holmes. Quotation: extract from *Esprit de Corps*, read by Norman Shelley.

December 1957. TP. "Poems by Seferis." Read in Greek and English by Elsa Verghis and Alan Wheatley. Translated by Lawrence Durrell and others.

28 December 1957. HS. "The Ghost Train," an episode from *Esprit de Corps*, read by Norman Shelley.

 7 June 1958. Net.3. "The World of Books: Library List." Paul Ferris comments on some recently published books, including *Balthazar*.

26 October 1958. HS. "The Critics." Review of *Mountolive* by Elspeth Huxley. [Repeated 30 October.]

21 December 1958. TP. "Work in Progress." John Bowen talks about *Mountolive* and its place in the group of novels on which

Lawrence Durrell is now working.

4 February 1960. TP. "Comment" [*Clea*].

6 February 1960. HS. "The World of Books."
Introduced by Robin Holmes [*Clea*].

19 April 1960. TP. "Into the Forties: A
Literary Miscellany." Compiled and
introduced by John Lehmann ["This Unimportant
Morning"].

14 May 1960. HS. "The World of Books."
Introduced by Robin Holmes. [*The Collected
Poems of Lawrence Durrell*, from which "Bitter
Lemons" was read.]

23 July 1960. HS. "The World of Books."
William Sansom talks on a subject chosen by
himself [*The Best of Henry Miller*, edited by
Lawrence Durrell.].

21 March 1961. Net.3. "Talking of Films:
Alexandria on Film." Lawrence Durrell, who
is working on the script of *Cleopatra*, talks
with Peter Duval Smith.

30 June 1962. HS. "The World of Books."
Introduced by Michael Vowden. *Penguin Modern
Poets, Volume I* reviewed by Lawrence Durrell.

24 August 1962. HS. "Readings on Record."
Introduced by J. W. Lambert. "Ballad of the
Oedipus Complex" and "La Rochefoucauld" read
by Lawrence Durrell.

8 October 1962. TP. "Discussion." Henry
Miller and Lawrence Durrell discuss their
writing with D. G. Bridson. [A conversation
recorded during the Writer's Conference,
Edinburgh, August 1962.]

21 January 1963. TP. "Conversations with
Lawrence Durrell," recorded in France by
D. G. Bridson. [The first of two programs.
The subjects covered in this conversation
include Lawrence Durrell's poetry, his books
on Corfu, Rhodes, Cyprus, and Alexandria, and
his preference for life near the Mediterranean.]

27 January 1963. TP. "Conversations with
Lawrence Durrell," recorded in France by
D. G. Bridson. [The second of two programs.
The subject of this conversation is mainly
The Alexandria Quartet. The author explains
the form of the work and his theories of
composition.]

29 January 1963. TP. Lawrence Durrell reading
a selection of his own poetry. Introduced
by D. G. Bridson.

 5 February 1963. TP. "Personal Anthology."
Lawrence Durrell introduces and discusses
poems of his own choice.

20 February 1963. TP. Extended version of
Writer's Conference program broadcast on
8 October 1962.

16 September 1963. HS. "For Schools: Prose and
Verse." "Night Fishing," from *Prospero's
Cell*.

20 January 1965. TP. "Islands." An examination
of some of those islands--real or imaginary,
geographical or symbolic--which have caught
the imagination of poets from Spenser to
Durrell. Program compiled and introduced by
Terence Tiller. ["Delos."]

 6 March 1967. LP. "Roundabout: Poets in Jazz."

10 April 1968. TP. "The Lively Arts." An

interview by George Fraser and Bolivar le
Franc regarding *Tunc*.

14 April 1968. R4. "The Critics." Discussion
of *Tunc*.

 8 May 1969. MP. "Music Making: Songs of
Lawrence Durrell."

15 December 1969. R4. *Acte* [adapted version].

25 March 1970. TP. "The Arts This Week."
Discussion with Anthony Bloomfield.

 4 July 1971. RL. Interview with Dennis Boyles.

 2 September 1972. "Woman's Hour." General
interview.

25 April 1973. "Today," about *The Black Book*.

28 April 1973. "Kaleidoscope," about *The Black
Book*.

31 July 1973. "Themes of Today" ["Delos"].

14 October 1974. "Kaleidoscope." Interview
about *Monsieur, or The Prince of Darkness*.

The following references are to French Radio.
Point of origin is shown for each program.

 1 February 1959. "Etranger Mon Ami," by
Dominic Arban.

 5 December 1959. Interview. Montpellier-
Languedoc.

 5 May 1962. Interview about a signing session.
Montpellier-Languedoc.

10 December 1963. "Un Corbeau de Toutes

Couleurs." Play from a novel by Claude
Seignolle. Forward by Durrell. Montpellier-
Languedoc.

11 February 1966. "Roy Campbell et la Provence."
Contribution by Durrell. Marseille-Provence.

Television

The following are B.B.C. Television appearances.

15 September 1959. "Interview."

14 February 1960. "Monitor." The poet and
novelist filmed at his home in the Camargue,
talking about his Alexandrian novels with
Huw Wheldon. [See Section H.: *Monitor: An
Anthology*, edited by Huw Wheldon (1962).]

 2 June 1960. "To-Night." British diplomats
abroad.

 7 August 1960. "Monitor: Summer Film Festival."
Selection from the first three years of
"Monitor. [See 14 February 1960, above.]

24 February 1961. "To-Night." Script for
Cleopatra.

 8 March 1961. "Wednesday Magazine."

 4 April 1961. "Insight." "The Vision of Our
Age," the final program in this series of
explorations into our new understanding of
nature. Dr. Bronowski discusses the
characteristic expression of insight and
imagination in the twentieth century with
Abdus Salam, Eduardo Paolozzi, Eero Saarinen,
and Lawrence Durrell. [See Section H.: J.
Bronowski, *Insight* (1964).]

11 June 1961. "Book Stand" [*The Alexandria
Quartet*].

22 August 1961. "To-Night."

19 October 1965. "Intimations." Interview with
Malcolm Muggeridge. Produced by Margaret
McCall.

27 October 1966. "Midday Dialogue." Lawrence
Durrell in his home in Provence comments on
his own poetry and engages in random
reflections. Durrell's poetry read by Marius
Goring. Produced by Margaret McCall.

28 October 1966. "Late Night Line-up."
Interview.

 1 November 1966. "Midday Dialogue." Poetry by
Durrell.

 2 March 1968. "Release." New Exhibition at
the Camden Arts Theatre. Interview.

 6 April 1968. "Release." Interviewed on *Tunc*.

17 May 1968. "Comedy Playhouse" [*Stiff Upper
Lip*].

17 May 1968. "Late Night Line-up" [*Tunc*].

11 May 1969. "Omnibus: Lawrence Durrell's
Paris."

21 March 1970. "The Lonely Roads," a study of
tramps and tramp lore in Provence, with Diane
Deriaz. In color. Produced by Margaret
McCall.

 9 July 1970. "Late Night Line-up: In Tribute
to John Gawsworth." [Repeated after
Gawsworth's death later in the year.]

25 July 1970. "Chronicle: The Alexandrians."
Written by Durrell.

2 May 1973. "Midweek." Interview about his latest book.

12 October 1973. "The Book Programme." Interview with Durrell about his life.

19 October 1974. "Parkinson." A wide-ranging interview prompted by the publication of *Monsieur, or The Prince of Darkness*.

13 March 1976. "Spirit of Place: Lawrence Durrell's Greece."

9 April 1978. "Spirit of Place: Lawrence Durrell's Egypt."

The following are French television appearances.

31 January 1964. "Chez Lawrence Durrell." Script by F.-J. Temple. Radio-Télévision Française, Ière chaîne.

February 1971. "Special sur Durrell." Produced by Michèle Arnaud. Paris ORTF.

The following are North American television appearances.

1968. "Telescope: Durrell by Himself," an interview with C.B.C. television for the series hosted by Fletcher Markle.

[n.d.]. "The Search for Ulysses," a color film based on the book by Ernley Bradford. Durrell appears to comment on Corfu and Ithaca. A C.B.C. presentation.

[n.d.]. A color film of Durrell showing Sophia Loren around places of interest in Israel was made for C.B.S. television during the filming of *Judith*. *"I acted her off her pretty little feet."*

Film

Durrell was commissioned to write a short story, on an Israeli theme, as the basis of a film for Sophia Loren. The script itself was arranged and expanded by other hands. Durrell comments: *"My first version did not please Miss Loren. She was scared of playing an atomic physicist because she said, with endearing frankness, that nobody would ever believe her as an intelligent woman; she was a* fille du peuple *and had learned not to try and operate outside her own natural limits, her* gamme. *I found her so worthy of respect that I tore up the version and did another on the spot. In order to please I accepted many ideas of which I did not approve from her literary adviser and from Unger, the producer. . . . I haven't seen the result yet, probably never will. I would have liked it to be good for Miss Loren's sake, but film is film, and the wise man takes his money and runs for it; which is what I did. No, I don't intend to publish in book form. Faulkner never published his movie scripts, why should I?"* [See Section E.: *Woman's Own* (26 February-2 April 1966).]

G. ANA

In Chronological Order

THE BOOSTER (Paris), II (October 1937).
    Contains Henry Miller, "A Boost for *The
    Black Book*."

T'IEN HSIA MONTHLY (Shanghai), VII: 4 (November
    1938). Contains a review of *The Black
    Book* by Emily Hahn.

Kahane, Jack. *MEMOIRS OF A BOOKLEGGER*. London:
    Michael Joseph, 1939. [Memoirs of the
    founder of The Obelisk Press, Paris,
    publisher of Henry Miller and of *The Black
    Book*.]

THE POETRY REVIEW (London), XXIV: 5/6 (September
    1943). Contains "Poets & Pretenders: A
    Faithful Survey of Contemporary
    Expressions," which includes a review of
    A Private Country.

Coward, Noel. *MIDDLE EAST DIARY*. London:
    Heinemann, 1944. ["August 22nd: The day
    broke fair and excessively warm but I
    didn't notice as I slept until twelve
    o'clock when, with my breakfast tray on
    my knees, I gave an interview to Larry
    Darrell (sic) who lived in Corfu and
    writes poems."]

---. New York: Doubleday, 1944.

POETRY (LONDON), X (1944). Edited by Tambimuttu.
London: Nicholson & Watson, 1944. Contains
Alan Ross, "The Poetry of Mnemotechny,"
and a review of *A Private Country*.

Treece, Henry. *HOW I SEE APOCALYPSE*. London:
Lindsay Drummond, 1946.

POETRY REVIEW (London) (May-June 1947). Contains
John Waller, "Lawrence Durrell: A Clever
Magician."

LEAVES IN THE STORM: A BOOK OF DIARIES. Edited
with a running commentary by Stefan
Schimanski and Henry Treece. London:
Lindsay Drummond, 1947. Contains John
Waller, "Athens in Spring" [Katsimbalis
and Durrell].

POETRY (LONDON), XII (November-December 1947).
Edited by Tambimuttu. Contains Hugh
Gordon Porteus, "Point of View: Three
Exiles."

Stanford, Derek. *THE FREEDOM OF POETRY: STUDIES
IN CONTEMPORARY VERSE*. London: The Falcon
Press, 1947. Contains a critical essay on
Durrell, with plate and select bibliography.

Leavis, Frank Raymond. *THE GREAT TRADITION*.
London: Chatto & Windus, 1948. Contains
"I have in mind writers in whom Mr. Eliot
has expressed an interest in strongly
favourable terms; . . . Henry Miller,
Lawrence Durrell of *The Black Book*. In
these writers. . . the spirit of what we
are offered affects me as being essentially
a desire, in Lawrentian phrase, to 'do
dirt' on life."

Morse, A. Reynolds. *THE WORKS OF M. P. SHIEL:
A STUDY IN BIBLIOGRAPHY*. Los Angeles:

Fantasy Publishing Co., 1948. Contains a
reproduction of the first proclamation of
Juan R., King of Redonda [John Gawsworth],
in which Durrell is appointed to "The
Duchy of Cervantes Pequena." The
proclamation is dated 29 June 1947.
[See A.46: *Spirit of Place*, "Some Notes
on My Friend John Gawsworth," which
mentions the appointment.]

Waller, John Stanier. *THE KISS OF STARS*.
London: Heinemann, 1948. Contains poem,
"Didcot." A note by the author: "This
parody of Durrell's "Nemea" was to have
appeared in a parody number of *Personal
Landscape* but the issue never
materialized."

ΕΦΗΜΕΡΙΣ ΤΩΝ ΕΙΔΗΣΕΩΝ [Daily Newspaper] (Athens)
(10 March 1950). Contains ῎Ενας ποιητὴς
μιλεῖ γιὰ τὴν Κέρκυρα ("A poet speaks
about Corfu."). Signed: M. I. Δ.

THE PENGUIN BOOK OF CONTEMPORARY VERSE. Edited
by Kenneth Allott. London: Penguin Books,
1950. Contains three poems and a
biocritical sketch. [See Section D.:
Item 18c.]

Powell, Lawrence Clark. *ISLANDS OF BOOKS*. Los
Angeles: The Ward Ritchie Press, 1951.
The title essay is partly devoted to
Durrell and his work.

Ross, Alan. *POETRY 1945-1950*. London: Longmans
Green for The British Council, 1951.
Contains "Mediterranean Littorals," a
discussion of Durrell, Bernard Spencer,
and Terence Tiller.

---. Folcroft, Pa.: Folcroft, 1974.

WORLD REVIEW (January 1952). Contains D. J.
     Enright, "The Cultural War: A Note on
     the Intelligentsia of Alexandria."

THE SPECTATOR (London), CXCI (21 August 1953).
     Contains Rex Warner, a review of
     Reflections on a Marine Venus.

NEW MEXICO QUARTERLY, XXIII (Autumn 1953).
     Contains Grover Smith, a review of *Key
     to Modern British Poetry*.

VOICES, No. 153 (January-April 1954). Contains
     Robert E. Stauffer, a review of *Key to
     Modern British Poetry*.

THE NEW STATESMAN AND NATION (London) (13
     October 1965). Contains G. S. Fraser,
     "Matter and Art."

POETRY (May 1954). Contains Babette Deutsch,
     a review of *Key to Modern British Poetry*.

IRISH WRITING, No. 32 (Autumn 1955). Edited by
     S. J. White. Contains Valentin Iremonger,
     a review of *The Tree of Idleness*.

Durrell, Gerald. *MY FAMILY AND OTHER ANIMALS*.
     London: Rupert Hart-Davis, 1956.

---. New York: Viking, 1957.

Also available as a talking book for the blind.

[A charming account of the idyllic life led by
the Durrell family in Corfu between the wars.
With an affectionate, if somewhat caricatured,
portrait of Lawrence Durrell as seen through the
eyes of a younger brother.]

THE LONDON MAGAZINE, IV: 2 (February 1957).
     Contains a review of *Selected Poems*.

THE NATION, CLXXIV (18 May 1957). Contains
 Kenneth Rexroth, "Footsteps of Horace."

ENCOUNTER (London), No. 45 (1957). Contains
 Burns Singer, a review of *Justine*.

GEMINI, I: 8 (Summer 1957). Contains Elizabeth
 Jennings, a review of *Justine*.

POETRY BROADSIDE, I: 2 (Summer 1957). Contains
 Barbara Clark, a review of *Selected Poems*.

THE LONDON MAGAZINE, IV: 10 (October 1957).
 Contains Bernard Spencer, a review of
 Bitter Lemons.

ENCOUNTER (London), No. 57 (1958). Contains
 John Mortimer, a review of *Balthazar*.

LES LETTRES NOUVELLES (Paris) (6 Fevrier 1958).
 Contains Robert Kemp, "Note."

---. (Fevrier 1958). Contains J. Howlet,
 "*Balthazar* de Lawrence Durrell."

LA NOUVELLE REVUE FRANCAISE (Paris) (Mars 1958).
 Contains Dominique Aury, "Note."

POETRY, XCI: 6 (March 1958). Contains Robert
 Stock, "Loneliness in the Isles of Greece."

REPORTER, XVIII (3 April 1958). Contains Gerald
 Sykes, "Electra Brought Him Black Roses."

NEW REPUBLIC, CXXVII (26 May 1958). Contains
 G. Merrick, "Will Lawrence Durrell Spoil
 America?"

THE TIMES LITERARY SUPPLEMENT (London), No.2,938
 (20 June 1958). Contains "The Experience
 of a Lifetime." Unsigned.

TIME (New York), LXXII (25 August 1958).
     Contains "Portrait."

ENCOUNTER (London), No. 63 (1958). Contains
     K. Gransden, review of *Mountolive*.

DIE WELT (Hamburg) (1 November 1958). Contains
     Willy Haas, "Durch die Höllen und
     Paradiese des Eros. Bezaubernd für Jeden,
     der Unterhaltung sucht--und dennoch
     Schaumgebäck."

FRANKFURTER ALLGEMEINE ZEITUNG (Frankfurt)
     (8 November 1958). Contains Wolfgang
     Schwerbrock, "Neue Dimensionen des
     modernen Romans? Lawrence Durrell:
     Justine."

DIE ZEIT (Hamburg) (21 November 1958). Contains
     Walter Jens, "Ein Anwärter auf den
     Nobelpreis. Das Preislied Alexandriens:
     bei aller Verworfenheit würdig und bei
     allem Wissen menschlich."

MERCURE DE FRANCE, No. 1143 (Novembre 1958).
     Contains Jacques Vallette, "Lettres Anglo-
     Saxonnes: *Justine, Balthazar* et Lawrence
     Durrell."

KOELNISCHE RUNDSCHAU (Köln) (28 Dezember 1958).
     Contains H. Olles, "Erfahrungen der Liebe.
     Der Roman *Justine* von Lawrence Durrell."

WIRTSCHAFTSZEITUNG (Stuttgart) (13 Januar 1959).
     Contains Oda Schaefer, "Orientalische
     Erotik. Lawrence Durrell: *Justine*."

*MERKUR: DEUTSCHE ZEITSCHRIFT FUR EUROPAISCHES
     DENKEN* (Stuttgart/Baden-Baden), XIII
     (Januar 1959). Contains Hans Magnus
     Enzensberger, "Die Haupstadt der
     Erinnerung."

KURIER (Berlin) (1 Februar 1959). Contains
	Hermann Linden, "Liebe in Alexandria.
	Lawrence Durrell: *Justine*."

TAGESSPIEGEL (Berlin) (1 Februar 1959).
	Contains Günter Blöcker, "Beschwörung
	einer Stadt. Zu Lawrence Durrells Roman
	Justine."

ARTS (Paris) (12 Fevrier 1959). Contains Michel
	Mohrt, "Note."

THE LONDON MAGAZINE (February 1959). Contains
	Frank Kermode, "Romantic Agonies."

POETRY, XCIII: 5 (February 1959). Contains
	Hayden Carruth, "'And I shal clynken yow
	so mery a belle that I shal wakyn al this
	companye.'"

BADISCHE NEUESTE NACHRICHTEN (Karlsruhe)
	(6 Marz 1959). Contains P. H., "Ein
	Anwärter auf den Nobelpreis. *Justine* von
	Lawrence Durrell."

DER TAG (Berlin) (8 Marz 1959). Contains Helmut
	Uhlig, "Ein Bohemien lebt gefährlich.
	Lawrence Durrell: *Justine*."

COMMONWEAL, LXX: 1 (3 April 1959). Contains
	Robert Gutwillig, "The Third Chapter in a
	Modern Literary Experiment," a review of
	Mountolive.

TWO CITIES--HOMMAGE A LAWRENCE DURRELL (Paris),
	I: 1 (15 Avril 1959). Contains Henry
	Miller, "The Durrell of the *Black Book*
	Days;" Alfred Perlès, "Enter Jupiter Jr.;"
	F.-J. Temple, "Construire un mur de pierre
	sèche;" Richard Aldington, "A Note on
	Lawrence Durrell," and Edwin Mullins, "On
	Mountolive."

DIE ZEIT (Hamburg) (17 April 1959). Contains
     Paul Hühnerfeld, "Neues aus der Welt der
     Justine. Auch der zweite Roman in
     Lawrence Durrells grosser Tetralogie
     bringt keine Erlösung."

FRANKFURTER ALLGEMEINE ZEITUNG (Frankfurt)
     (18 April 1959). Contains Günter Blöcker,
     "Der vieldimensionale Erzähler. Lawrence
     Durrell: *Balthazar*."

TAGESSPIEGEL (Berlin) (26 April 1959). Contains
     Günter Blöcker, "Alles über Justine.
     Lawrence Durrell: *Balthazar*." [Slightly
     changed and abridged from *Frankfurter
     Allgemeine Zeitung* (18 April 1959).]

L'EXPRESS (Paris) (7 Mai 1959). Contains
     François Erval, "Note."

L'OBSERVATEUR LITTERAIRE (Paris) (7 Mai 1959).
     Contains Claude Roy, "Note."

THE LISTENER (London), LXI: 1,578 (25 June
     1959). Contains Karl Miller, "Poets'
     Novels," discussing Durrell and others.

DER ROMANFUEHRER, X. Stuttgart: Hiersemann,
     1959. Contains Jurgen Eyssen, *"Justine."*

KULTUR (München), VII (1958-1959). Contains
     Fritz J. Raddatz, "Der Roman als
     Antiroman? Bemerkungen zu Lawrence
     Durrell."

DIE WELT (Hamburg) (25 Juli 1959). Contains
     Jost Nolte, "Die literarischen Zaubereien
     des Lawrence Durrell. Der zweite Roman
     Balthazar des vieldiskutierten irischen
     Autors liegt vor."

L'ARC: CAHIERS MEDITERRANEENS (Aix-en-Provence),

2e année, No. 7 (Juillet 1959). Contains
François Erval, "Lawrence Durrell."
Portrait.

SOUTHWEST REVIEW, XLIV: 3 (Summer 1959).
Contains Mary Graham Lund, "Submerge for
Reality: The New Novel Form of Lawrence
Durrell."

THE TIMES LITERARY SUPPLEMENT (London),
No. 2,997 (7 August 1959). Contains John
Bowen, "One Man's Meat: The Idea of
Individual Responsibility." Portrait.

WELT UND WORT (Tübingen) (August 1959).
Contains Anna Ozana, "Auf dem Weg zum
modernen Roman. Gedanken bei der Lektüre
der Roman Lawrence Durrells."

DER TAG (Berlin) (6 September 1959). Contains
Helmut Uhlig, "Roman in vier Stockwerken.
Zu Lawrence Durrells *Balthazar*."

NEWS CHRONICLE (London) (9 September 1959).
Contains David Holloway, "Why Mr. Durrell
Can't Afford to Write Poetry." [Interview.]

KURIER (Berlin) (30 Oktober 1959). Contains
Heino Heinen, "Balthazars lästiges
Drehkreuz. Lawrence Durrell: *Balthazar*."

FRANKFURTER ALLGEMEINE ZEITUNG (Frankfurt)
(23 November 1959). Contains Klaus
Wagner, "Liebe und Tod auf Lesbos.
Gründgens inszeniert Durrells *Sappho* in
Deutsches Schauspielhaus Hamburg."

DIE WELT (Hamburg) (23 November 1959). Contains
Willy Haas, "Traum von der Inselwelt des
alten Griechenland. Kein Drama, ein
Gedicht: Lawrence Durrells *Sappho*
uraufgeführt."

Also contains W[illy] H[aas], "Ein Ire,
der Hellas sucht. Interview mit Lawrence
Durrell."

DER TAG (Berlin) (24 November 1959). Contains
Claus Henning Bachmann, "Koloss für
Feinschmecker. Lawrence Durrells *Sappho*
bei Gründgens uraufgeführt."

TAGESSPEIGEL (Berlin) (24 November 1959).
Contains Johannes Jacobi, "Irische
Uraufführung bei Gustav Gründgens.
Lawrence Durrells *Sappho* mit Elisabeth
Flickenschildt im Hamburger Deutschen
Schauspielhaus."

DIE ZEIT (Hamburg) (27 November 1959). Contains
D[ieter E.] Z[immer], "Ein Abend mit
Lawrence Durrell."

RHEINISCHER MERKUR (Koblenz), No. 48 (1959).
Contains Heinz Beckmann, "Sapphos Tochter
weint. Lawrence Durrell begann bei
Gründgens als Dramatiker."

DER SPIEGEL (Hamburg), XIII: 49 (2 Dezember
1959). Contains "Durrell. Inselsucht,"
in the "Dichter" series.

LES LETTRES FRANCAIS (Paris) (17 Decembre 1959).
Contains Hubert Juin, "Paroles avec
Lawrence Durrell."

ENCOUNTER (London), XIII: 6 (December 1959).
Contains Kenneth Young, "A Dialogue with
Durrell."

DER MONAT: EINE INTERNATIONALE ZEITSCHRIFT
(Berlin/Frankfurt), XII: 135 (Dezember
1959). Contains Walter Schurenberg,
"Lawrence Durrell als Dramatiker."

EPOCH, IX (Winter 1959). Contains William
      Righter, a review of *Justine*, *Balthazar*,
      and *Mountolive*.

PARIS REVIEW, No. 22 (Autumn-Winter 1959-60).
      Contains Julian Mitchell and Gene
      Andrewski, "The Art of Fiction, XXXIII:
      Lawrence Durrell," an interview with
      Durrell in Provence. [See *Writers at
      Work* (1963), below.]

DIE VOLKSBUEHNE (Hamburg), X (1959-60).
      Contains G. Penzoldt, "Uber Lawrence
      Durrell und seine *Sappho*."

DIE WELT (Hamburg) (21 Januar 1960). Contains
      D. W., "Von Sonnabend an neuer Roman.
      Lawrence Durrell: *Mountolive*." With a
      photograph of Durrell signing books in a
      Hamburg bookshop. [Announces the
      forthcoming serialization of *Mountolive*
      in *Die Welt*.]

BOOKS AND BOOKMEN (London), V: 5 (February
      1960). Contains W[illiam] G. S[mith],
      "Lawrence Durrell: Is He the Only Great
      Novelist of the Fifties?" Two portraits.
      [Interview.]

THE TIMES LITERARY SUPPLEMENT (London),
      No. 3,023 (5 February 1960). Contains
      "Time Released." Unsigned.

THE NEW STATESMAN (London), LIX (13 February
      1960). Contains V. S. Pritchett, a
      review of *The Alexandria Quartet*.

JOHN O'LONDON'S WEEKLY, II: 20 (18 February
      1960). Contains R. G. Thomas, "Durrell
      Rounds It Off," a review of *Clea*.
      Portrait.

THE SPECTATOR (London), CCIV (19 February 1960).
Contains John Coleman, "Mr. Durrell's
Dimensions."

THE OBSERVER (London) (28 February 1960).
Contains "Profile: Lawrence Durrell."
Portrait.

NEUE ZUERCHER ZEITUNG (Zürich) (19 Marz 1960).
Contains O. S., "Lawrence Durrell."

HORIZON (London), II: 4 (March 1960). Contains
Gilbert Highet, "The Alexandrians of
Lawrence Durrell."

TWENTIETH CENTURY, CLXVII: 997 (March 1960).
Contains Cecily Mackworth, "Lawrence
Durrell and the New Romanticism."

DIE ZEIT (Hamburg) (1 April 1960). Contains
Paul Hühnerfeld, "Aller guten Dinge sind
vier. Der dritte Band von Lawrence
Durrells grosser Roman-Tetralogie gibt
Anlass zu Hoffnungen und Befürchtungen."

TIME (New York), LXXV (4 April 1960). Contains
"Carnal Jigsaw." Unsigned.

CHRIST UND WELT (Stuttgart) (28 April 1960).
Contains Giselher Wirsing, "Der grosse
Roman der Levante. Das Werk von Lawrence
Durrell." Portrait.

REVIEW OF ENGLISH LITERATURE, I: 2 (April
1960). Contains Frank Kermode, "Fourth
Dimension," on *The Alexandria Quartet*.

AMBIT (Spring 1960). Contains Martin Bax,
"A Total War," a comment on *The Alexandria
Quartet*.

THE BOOK COLLECTOR (London), IX: 1 (Spring 1960).

Contains Alan G. Thomas and Lawrence
Clark Powell, "Some Uncollected Authors,
XXIII: Lawrence Durrell--Recollections of
a Durrell Collector."

TWO CITIES (Paris) (15 May 1960). Contains
Dylan Thomas, "Letters to Lawrence
Durrell."

THE DAILY TELEGRAPH (London) (13 May 1960).
Contains Kenneth Young, "Durrell and
Plomer," a review of *Collected Poems*.
Portrait.

FRANKFURTER ALLGEMEINE ZEITUNG (Frankfurt)
(14 Mai 1960). Contains Günter Blöcker,
"Das Blatt ist mehrfach beschrieben.
Lawrence Durrell: *Mountolive*." [See
Tagesspiegel (29 Mai 1960), below.]

DER TAG (Berlin) (22 Mai 1960). Contains
Helmut Uhlig, "Ein Roman von Weltrang.
Zu Lawrence Durrells *Mountolive*."

TAGESSPIEGEL (Berlin) (29 Mai 1960). Contains
Günter Blöcker, "Das Blatt ist mehrfach
beschrieben. Lawrence Durrell:
Mountolive." [Slightly abridged from
Frankfurter Allgemeine Zeitung (14 Mai
1960).]

CRITIQUE (Paris), XVI: 156 (Mai 1960). Contains
Jean-Paul Hamard, "L'Espace et le Temps
dans les Romans de Lawrence Durrell."

ENCOUNTER (London), XIV: 5 (May 1960). Contains
Hilary Corke, "Mr. Durrell and Brother
Criticus."

WELT UND WORT: LITERARISCHE MONATSSCHRIFT
(Tübingen), XV: 5 (Mai 1960). Contains
Anna Ozana, "Enttäuschung über Durrell."

THE NATION, No. 190 (4 June 1960). Contains "What is Wrong with Durrell?" Unsigned, but by Kenneth Rexroth.

YALE REVIEW, XLIX: 4 (June 1960). Contains George Steiner, "Lawrence Durrell: The Baroque Novel," and Martin Green, "Lawrence Durrell: A Minority Report."

DIETSCHE WARANDE EN BELFORT, CV (1960). Contains M. Engelborghs, "Engelse Letteren. Nieuwe Engelse Romankunst: Lawrence Durrell."

Powell, Lawrence Clark. *BOOKS IN MY BAGGAGE*. London: Constable, 1960.

PREUVES, No. 109 (1960). Contains Dominic Arban, "Lawrence Durrell."

PUNCH (London), No. 238 (1960). Contains Peter Dickinson, "A Clutch of Poets."

REVUE DES LANGUES VIVANTES, XXVI: 5 (1960). Contains Paulette Michot, "Lawrence Durrell's *Alexandria Quartet*."

Rodis, Roufos. *THE AGE OF BRONZE*. London: Heinemann, 1960. [A novel about the Cyprus troubles by a Greek diplomat. In an earlier version, there is a recognizable portrait of Durrell as Maurice Ferrell, a poet (author of *Sour Grapes* and *The Bench of Idleness*), who is working as Information Officer. In the published version, this character appears as Harry Montague, and much of the resemblance to Durrell has been discarded.]

SAMTIDEN: TIDSSKRIFT FOR POLITIKK, LITTERATUR OG SAMFUNNSSPORSMAL, LXIX: 9 (1960). Contains Ragnar Kvam, "Ny Engelsk Prosa,"

discussing Durrell, C. P. Snow, and
Colin Wilson.

VINDUET, XIV (1960). Contains Ragnar Kvam,
"Lawrence Durrell."

REVUE NOUVELLE, XXXI: 7 (15 Juillet 1960).
Contains Franz Weyergans, "*Clea* by
Lawrence Durrell."

INTERNATIONALES BIOGRAPHISCHES ARCHIV [*MUNZINGER
ARCHIV*] (16 Juli 1960). Contains
"Lawrence Durell (sic), Britischer
Schriftsteller und Diplomat." [Revised
editions 21 Mai 1966, 30 April 1971, and
11 Marz 1978.]

TIME (New York), LXXVI (18 July 1960). Contains
"On the Volcano."

MERCURE DE FRANCE, No. 1163 (Juillet 1960).
Contains Jacques Vallette, "Lettres
Anglo-Saxonnes: Note sur *Clea*."

LIBERTE, LX (Mai-Août 1960). Contains P.
Trottier, "Lawrence Durrell."

MAGNUM (Köln) (2 August 1960). Contains H. L.
Tank, "Autoren die im Gespräch sind:
Lawrence Durrell."

THE NEW YORKER, XXXVI: 26 (13 August 1960).
Contains Naomi Bliven, "Books: Alexandrine
in Tetrameter."

BERLINER MORGENPOST (Berlin) (11 September 1960).
Contains Kurt Lamerdin, "Liebe und
Diplomatie. Zu Lawrence Durrells neuem
Roman *Mountolive*."

ESQUIRE (New York) (September 1960). Contains
Thomas B. Morgan, "The Autumnal Arrival

of Lawrence Durrell."

GRIFFIN, IX: 9 (September 1960). Contains Kenneth Rexroth, "The Art of Convincing Immodesty."

COLUMBIA UNIVERSITY FORUM (New York), III: 4 (Fall 1960). Contains Erik Wensberg, "I've Been Reading."

HUDSON REVIEW, XIII: 3 (Autumn 1960). Contains Benjamin DeMott, "Grading the Emanglons."

DER TAG (Berlin) (2 November 1960). Contains Claus Henning Bachmann, "So sauber die Worte gesetzt waren. . . Heinz Hilpert inszeniert Durrells *Sappho* in Göttingen."

LIFE (New York), XLIX: 21 (21 November 1960). Contains Nigel Dennis, "New Four-Star King of Novelists."

RÉALITES (Paris), No. 178 (Novembre 1960). Contains "Lawrence Durrell Vous Parle," an interview accompanied by a passage from *Acte*.

PARIS MATCH, No. 608 (3 Decembre 1960). Contains Guillaume Hanoteau, "Lawrence Durrell, riche et glorieux grâce à quatre femmes, se carré de dames apporte la gloire et la fortune à ce poète inconnu." Illustrated.

CRITIQUE (Paris), XVI: 163 (Decembre 1960). Contains Jean-Paul Hamard, "Lawrence Durrell, Renovateur Assagi."

CAHIERS DU SUD, L: 38 (Decembre 1960-Janvier 1961). Contains Raymond Jean, "Lawrence Durrell ou le Temps délivré."

DER ABEND (Berlin) (7 Januar 1961). Contains
     "Roman unter Oliven. Der beschwerliche
     Weg des Lawrence Durrell." Portrait.

LIFE (New York), L (27 January 1961). Contains
     "Durrell Reunion at the Family Zoo."
     Portraits.

CITE LIBRE, II (January 1961). Contains P.
     Laberge, "Bien-Aimée Alexandria."

LITERARY HALF-YEARLY, II: 1 (January 1961).
     Contains Hilary Corke, "Lawrence Durrell."

JOHN O'LONDON'S, IV: 72 (16 February 1961).
     Contains Carl Bode, "Lawrence Durrell."

DELTA, No. 23 (February 1961). Contains
     Richard Boston, "Some Notes on *The
     Alexandria Quartet*."

ΕΙΚΟΝΕΣ (Athens), No. 282 (17 March 1961).
     Contains Ἕνας μεγάλος μυθιδτοριογράφος
     ἀνατέλλει (A Great Novelist Rises).
     Illustrated. [Also published in English
     as *Pictures from Greece*.]

DIE WELT (Hamburg) (22 Marz 1961). Contains
     Jost Nolte, "Zum vierten und letzten Mal
     Alexandria. Mit *Clea* ist die gross
     angelegte Tetralogie von Lawrence Durrell
     beendet."

SEWANEE REVIEW (Sewanee, Tennessee), LXIX: 1
     (January-March 1961). Contains Bonamy
     Dobree, "Durrell's Alexandrian Series."

FRANKFURTER ALLGEMEINE ZEITUNG (Frankfurt)
     (22 April 1961). Contains Günter Blöcker,
     "Schussgalopp in der vierten Dimension."
     [Also printed in *Tagesspiegel* (21 Mai
     1961).]

POETRY, XCVIII: 1 (April 1961). Contains Charles
    Tomlinson, "And the Eyelids are a Little
    Weary."

REALITES (New York), No. 125 (April 1961).
    Contains "Lawrence Durrell: An Exclusive
    Interview." [A shortened form of the
    interview which appeared in *Realites*
    (Paris), No. 178 (Novembre 1960); see
    above.]

*PAPERS OF THE BIBLIOGRAPHICAL SOCIETY OF
    AMERICA*, LV: 2 (Second Quarter 1961).
    Contains Anthony Knerr, "Regarding a
    Checklist of Lawrence Durrell."

AUDIENCE, VIII: 2 (Spring 1961). Contains an
    unsigned review of *Collected Poems*.

THE GUARDIAN (Manchester) (6 May 1961). Contains
    W. J. Weatherby, "The Durrell Brothers."
    Illustrated.

COLLEGE ENGLISH, XXII (8 May 1961). Contains
    Carl Bode, "Durrell's Way to Alexandria."

BERLINER MORGENPOST (Berlin) (11 Mai 1961).
    Contains H. G., "Clea brachte die innere
    Wandlung. Der letzte Roman von Lawrence
    Durrells Alexandria Quartett."

TAGESSPIEGEL (Berlin) (21 Mai 1961). Contains
    Günter Blöcker, "Schussgalopp in der
    vierten Dimension." [See *Frankfurter
    Allgemeine Zeitung* (22 April 1961),
    above.]

DER TAG (Berlin) (4 June 1961). Contains Helmut
    Uhlig, "Finale in Alexandria. Lawrence
    Durrells Tetralogie ist abgeschlossen."

THE EVENING STANDARD (London) (20 June 1961)

Contains Richard Lister, a review of *The Alexandria Quartet.*

BOOKS AND BOOKMEN (London) (June 1961).
Contains Adrian Stockton, "Books that Shocked, 21: *The Black Book*."

CRITIQUE (Minneapolis), IV: 2 (Spring-Summer 1961). Contains Matthew N. Proser, "Darley's Dilemma: The Problem of Structure in Durrell's *Alexandria Quartet*," and Frank Baldanza, "Durrell's Word Continuum."

THE ANTIOCH REVIEW, XXI: 2 (Summer 1961).
Contains Mary Graham Lund, "The Alexandria Projection."

INTERNATIONAL LITERARY ANNUAL (London), III (1961). Contains D. J. Enright, "Alexandrian Night's Entertainment."

Jennings, Elizabeth. *POETRY TO-DAY*. London: Longmans Green for The British Council and The National Book League, 1961. Portrait.

Perlès, Alfred. *MY FRIEND LAWRENCE DURRELL*. With a Bibliography by Bernard Stone. Northwood, Middlesex: The Scorpion Press, 1961.

---. Also an edition specially bound, limited to 50 copies signed by the author.

---. London: Village Press, 1973. Paperback. [This edition lacks the bibliography by Bernard Stone.]

Potter, Robert A., and Brooke Whiting. *LAWRENCE DURRELL: A CHECKLIST*. Los Angeles: Library of the University of California at Los Angeles, 1961. "Issued

on the occasion of the presentation of
Lawrence Clark Powell's Durrell collection
to the UCLA Library in honor of his
successor as University Librarian, Robert
Vosper, and of an exhibit at the Library
of materials selected from the collection."
Also contains Lawrence Clark Powell, "On
Collecting Lawrence Durrell."

Rexroth, Kenneth. *ASSAYS*. Norfolk, Conn.:
New Directions, 1961. Contains "Lawrence
Durrell."

TERZO PROGRAMMA, No. 1 (1961). Contains
Agostino Lombardo, "Il Quartetto di
Alessandria."

DIE WELT (Hamburg) (28 Juli 1961). Contains
Willy Haas, "Was weiss man schon von dem
Geheimnis. . . Reisenotizen." [On *Bitter
Lemons*.]

THE SCOTSMAN (Edinburgh) (23 August 1961).
Contains an unsigned review of *Sappho*.

THE OBSERVER (London) (27 August 1961). Contains
Kenneth Tynan, "Durrell in Three
Dimensions," a review of *Sappho*.

THE SUNDAY TIMES (London) (27 August 1961).
Contains Harold Hobson, "The Quick and
the Dead," a review of *Sappho*.

STIMMEN DER ZEIT (Freiburg) (August 1961).
Contains Hubert Becher, "Lawrence Durrells
Tetralogie und die literarische Kritik."

CHRIST UND WELT (Stuttgart) (4 September 1961).
Contains Christa Rotzoll, "Unfug in Rom.
Lawrence Durrells *Actis* bei Gründgens in
Hamburg uraufgeführt."

TIME (New York), LXXVIII (8 September 1961).
Contains "Marine Justine." Unsigned.

KURIER (Berlin) (14 September 1961). Contains
Siegfried Kühn, "Der irische Erfolgsautor
schreibt ein Faust-Drama. Dreissig Jahre
Feigheit hinter sich: Lawrence Durrell."
[Interview with Durrell in Paris.]

VENTURE, II: 3/4 (September-December 1961).
Contains Michael Millgate, "Contemporary
English Fiction: Some Observations."

THE EVENING STANDARD (London) (5 October 1961).
Contains "Lawrence Durrell by His Brother
Gerald," No. 4 in a series of brotherly
articles. (Tomorrow: Robert Graves by his
brother Charles.) [Also appeared in *The
Manchester Evening Chronicle* on the same
date.]

COLLEGE ECHOES (October 1961). Contains an
unsigned review of the performance of
Sappho at the Edinburgh Festival.

FRANKFURTER ALLGEMEINE ZEITUNG (Frankfurt)
(24 November 1961). Contains Dieter
Hildebrandt, "Verstrickte Werke. Lawrence
Durrells *Actis* in Hamburg uraufgeführt."
With a photograph from the Hamburg
production showing Werner Hinz as Nero
and Joana Maria Gorvin as Actis.

DIE WELT (Hamburg) (24 November 1961). Contains
Willy Haas, "Neros Greuel--da kennen wir
ganz andere. Grosse Oper--Psychologisches
Drama: Lawrence Durrells *Actis* bei
Gründgens uraufgeführt." With a
photograph of Werner Hinz and Joana Maria
Gorvin from the Hamburg production.

TELEGRAF (Berlin) (25 November 1961). Contains

Alfred Gajewski, "Der Mensch ist gefangen!
Uraufführung von Lawrence Durrells *Actis*
in Hamburg."

KURIER (Berlin) (27 November 1961). Contains
Gerd Vielhaber, "Lawrence Durrells neues
Drama bei Gründgens uraufgeführt. Diese
Actis ist aus gröberem Stoff."

NEUE ZUERCHER ZEITUNG (Zürich) (27 November
1961). Contains G. Sch., "*Actis*.
Uraufführung in Hamburg."

WIRTSCHAFTSZEITUNG (Stuttgart) (27 November
1961). Contains Hans Daiber, "*Actis*.
Uraufführung in Hamburg."

TAGESSPIEGEL (Berlin) (28 November 1961).
Contains Johannes Jacobi, "Werkstattarbeit
Durrell-Gründgens. *Actis*--Uraufführung
im Deutschen Schauspielhaus in Hamburg."

SPANDAUER VOLKSBLATT (Berlin/Spandau)
(29 November 1961). Contains Walter
Weyer, "Dramatik und Drastik in Versen.
Lawrence Durrells Schauspiel *Actis* bei
Gründgens uraufgeführt."

DER SPIEGEL (Hamburg), XV: 49 (29 November 1961).
Contains "Theatre. Durrell-Premiere. Ja
zum Leben." With photographs of Durrell
with Gründgens, and, from the Hamburg
production, Joana Maria Gorvin as Actis
and Max Eckard as Fabius.

DER TAG (Berlin) (29 November 1961). Contains
Claus Henning Bachmann, "Wahreit im
Lächeln des Astheten. Gustav Gründgens
inszeniert Lawrence Durrells *Actis* im
Schauspielhaus."

DIE ZEIT (Hamburg) (1 Dezember 1961). Contains

Johannes Jacobi, "Der Alexandriner und der Klassizist. Zur Uraufführung von Lawrence Durrells poetischem Drama *Actis* am Hamburger Schauspielhaus." With a photograph from the Hamburg production of Joana Maria Gorvin as Actis and Max Eckard as Fabius.

DIE WELT (Hamburg) (6 Dezember 1961). Contains Christian Ferber, a review of *Ein Henry Miller Lesebuch*.

DIE ZEIT (Hamburg) (8 Dezember 1961). Contains Johannes Jacobi, "Ohne Gründgens kein Durrell. Vergleich zweier Permieren." [Compares the production of *Actis* in Hamburg by Gründgens with that in Göttingen by Hilpert.]

ATLANTIC MONTHLY (Boston), CCVIII: 6 (December 1961). Contains Curtis Cate, "Lawrence Durrell." Cover portrait in color.

MINNESOTA REVIEW, I (Winter 1961). Contains W. J. Wallace, a review of *The Alexandria Quartet*.

WATERLOO REVIEW, VI (Winter 1961). Contains R. A. O'Brien, "Time, Space and Language in Lawrence Durrell."

GYMNASIUM HELVETICUM (Aarau), XVI: 6 (1961-62). Contains Robert Fricker, "Lawrence Durrell: *The Alexandria Quartet*."

PRAIRIE SCHOONER, XXXV: 4 (Winter 1961-62). Contains Mary Graham Lund, "Durrell: Soft Focus on Crime."

THE SPECTATOR (London) (19 January 1962). Contains Sarah Gainham, "Durrell & Co.," a review of the Hamburg production of *Acte*.

THEATER HEUTE (Hanover) (Januar 1962). Contains
"Gründgens lasst Durrell hinter sich,"
illustrated; "Ein Briefwechsel über das
Drama *Actis*" (with Gustaf Gründgens); and
"*Actis*, Drama in drei Akten von Lawrence
Durrell" (German text of the play). [For
a finely printed edition of one item in
this issue, see Section A.35.]

GRANTA (Cambridge), LXV: 1215 (February 1962).
Contains Tony Tanner, "Lawrence Durrell."

BERLINER MORGENPOST (Berlin) (1 Marz 1962).
Contains Horst Windelboth, "Viel Lärm um
Actis. Theatersprung in die Hansestadt
Hamburg."

NEUER ZUERCHER ZEITUNG (Zürich) (25 Marz 1962).
Contains Dominik Jost, "Lawrence Durrell:
Das Alexandria Quartet."

THE SUNDAY TIMES COLOUR SECTION (London)
(18 March 1962). Contains Joyce Emerson,
"A New *Faust* from Durrell." Illustrated.

THE ATLANTIC (Boston), CCIX: 2 (March 1962).
Contains a note clarifying the role of
Durrell's American publisher, Dutton, in
the publication of *Justine*--a follow-up
to Curtis Cate's article in the December
1961 issue.

ETUDES ANGLAISES, XV: 2 (April-June 1962).
Contains Mahmoud Manzalaoui, "Curate's
Egg: An Alexandrian Opinion of Durrell's
Quartet."

LE MIDI LIBRE (3 Mai 1962). Contains F.-J.
Temple, "Lawrence Durrell Parmi Nous."

TELEGRAF (Berlin) (6 Mai 1962). Contains H. G.
Sellenthin, "Brennpunkte: Zypern und

Barcelona. Meisterhaftes von Durrell und Hortelano."

FOUR QUARTERS, XI: 4 (May 1962). Contains Mary Graham Lund, "The Big Rock Crystal Mountain."

TAGESSPIEGEL (Berlin) (6 Juni 1962). Contains Günter Blöcker, "Abschied eines Dichters von Cypern. Lawrence Durrell: *Bittere Limonen*."

ANGLO-SOVIET JOURNAL, XXXIII: 2 (Summer 1962). Contains I. Levidova, "A 'Four-Decker' in Stagnant Waters." [Levidova, irritated by the acclaim which the *Quartet* had received from the "bourgeois press," described it as a "vividly painted" ship unable to set sail.]

Foley, Charles. *ISLAND IN REVOLT*. London: Longmans, 1962. Illustrated. [An account of the Cyprus troubles, with several references to Durrell.]

---. Revised edition. Harmondsworth, Middlesex: Penguin Books, 1964.

GYMNASIUM HELVETICUM, XVI: 6 (1962). Contains Robert Fricker, "Lawrence Durrell: *The Alexandria Quartet*."

Karl, Frederick R. *THE CONTEMPORARY ENGLISH NOVEL*. New York: Farrar, Strauss & Cudahy, 1962. Contains "Lawrence Durrell: Physical and Metaphysical Love."

---. London: Thames and Hudson, 1963.

---. Revised edition: *A READER'S GUIDE TO THE CONTEMPORARY ENGLISH NOVEL*. New York: Farrar, Strauss & Giroux, 1972. [Adds a

highly critical discussion of *Tunc* and
Nunquam in "Postscript: 1960-1970."]

Kazin, Alfred. *CONTEMPORARIES*. Boston: Little,
    Brown, 1962. Contains "Lawrence Durrell's
    Rosy-Finger'd Egypt."

Kermode, Frank. *PUZZLES AND EPIPHANIES*. New
    York: Chilmark Press, 1962.

Mayer, Hans. *ANSICHTEN ZUR LITERATUR DER ZEIT*.
    Hamburg: Rowholt Verlag, 1962. Contains
    "Lawrence Durrell oder Proust in
    Alexandria."

MONITOR: AN ANTHOLOGY. Edited by Huw Wheldon.
    London: Macdonald, 1962. Illustrated.
    Contains an interview with Durrell.

NYA ARGUS, LV (1962). Contains Christer
    Kihlman, "Lawrence Durrell och den Moderna
    Romanen."

THE PERSONALIST, XLIII (1962). Contains John
    Arthos, "Lawrence Durrell's Gnosticism."

IL PONTE, XVIII: 1 (1962). Contains Alessandro
    Serpieri, "Il Quartetto di Alessandria di
    Lawrence Durrell."

*SAMTIDEN: TIDSSKRIFT FOR POLITIKK, LITTERATUR
    OG SAMFUNNSSPORSMAL*, LXXI (1962). Contains
    Ingvar Hauge, "Lawrence Durrell fram til
    Aleksandriakvartetten."

*SIX CONTEMPORARY NOVELS: SIX INTRODUCTORY ESSAYS
    IN MODERN FICTION*. Edited by William O.
    Sutherland, Jr. Austin: Humanities
    Research Centre, University of Texas,
    1962. Contains Ambrose Gordon, Jr.,
    "Time, Space, and Eros: The *Alexandria
    Quartet* Rehearsed."

THE WORLD OF LAWRENCE DURRELL.   Edited by Harry
     T. Moore.   Carbondale: Southern Illinois
     University Press, 1962.   Contains essays
     by seventeen authors; "Durrell Answers a
     Few Questions;" "The Kneller Tape
     (Hamburg);" Durrell, "Letters to Jean
     Fanchette."

---.   New York: E. P. Dutton, 1964.   Paperback.

---.   Toronto: Clarke, Irwin & Co., 1964.
     Paperback.

SUEDDEUTSCHE ZEITUNG (München) (14 Juli 1962).
     Contains Günter Blöcker, "Abschied eines
     Dichters von Cypern.   Lawrence Durrell:
     Bittere Limonen."   [Reprinted from
     Tagesspiegel (3 Juni 1962).]

THE SCOTSMAN (Edinburgh) (21 August 1962).
     Contains photograph of Lawrence Durrell
     conversing with Henry Miller at The
     Writers Conference, Edinburgh Festival.
     [The conference was widely reported in
     British newspapers and magazines during
     this week.]

EXPLICATOR, XXI: 1 (September 1962).   Contains
     Norman Silverstein and Arthur L. Lewis,
     "Durrell's 'Song for Zarathustra'."

COLLEGE ENGLISH, XXIV: 1 (October 1962).
     Contains Eleanor Hutchens, "The Heraldic
     Universe in *The Alexandria Quartet.*"

DER TAG (Berlin) (28 Oktober 1962).   Contains
     Wolfgang Kraus, "Stürmisch wilder Aufbruch.
     Zu Lawrence Durrells Roman *Die Schwarze
     Chronik.*"

REVUE GENERALE BELGE (Octobre 1962).   Contains
     Albert Gérard, "Lawrence Durrell, Un Grand
     Talent de Basse Epoque."

ΕΙΚΟΝΕΣ (Athens), No. 368 (9 November 1962).
    Contains Λώρενσ Ντάρρελ: "Μαγεία ἡ
    Ἑλλάδα!" Illustrated.

---. *Pictures from Greece*, No. 84 (January
    1963). Contains "Lawrence Durrell,
    Enchanted to be back in Greece!"
    Illustrated. [English version of the
    Εικονεσ article.]

TELEGRAF (Berlin) (11 November 1962). Contains
    Ingeborg Keller, "Am Anfang war der Zorn.
    Zu Lawrence Durrells *Schwarzer Chronik.*"

NEUER ZUERCHER ZEITUNG (Zürich) (13 November
    1962). Contains D[ominik] J[ost],
    "Lawrence Durrells *Schwarze Chronik.*"

FRANKFURTER ALLGEMEINE ZEITUNG (Frankfurt)
    (20 November 1962). Contains Günter
    Blöcker, "Der erste Schrei. Lawrence
    Durrell: *Die schwarze Chronik.*"

MOTIVE, No. 23 (November 1962). Contains David
    Littlejohn, "Lawrence Durrell, the
    Novelist as Entertainer."

DIE ZEIT (Hamburg) (November 1962). Contains
    Reinhard Baumgard, "Mit einem Mund voll
    Tinte. Lawrence Durrell mit
    fünfundzwanzig Jahren."

TAGESSPIEGEL (Berlin) (9 Dezember 1962).
    Contains Günter Blöcker, "Der erste Schrei
    Lawrence Durrells. Pflichtlektüre an einem
    Erstling." [Reprinted from *Frankfurter
    Allgemeine Zeitung* (20 November 1962).]

STUTTGARTER ZEITUNG (Stuttgart) (17 Dezember
    1962). Contains Rolf Michaelis, "Ausbruch
    eines Literatur-Vesuvs. Die deutsche
    Ausgabe von Lawrence Durrells erstem Roman
    Die schwarze Chronik."

FORUM (University of Houston), III: 9 (Winter 1962). Contains Mary Graham Lund, "Eight Aspects of Melissa: An Air of Mystery."

BALL STATE TEACHER'S COLLEGE FORUM, III: 2 (Winter 1962-63). Contains Richard Crowder, "Durrell, *Libido*, and *Eros*."

ACTUELLES, No. 1 (Janvier 1963). Contains F.-J. Temple, "Avec Lawrence Durrell." Illustrated.

SATURDAY REVIEW, XLVI (23 February 1963). Contains E. Moon, "From the Twosome a Quartet."

TIME (New York), LXXXI (1 March 1963). Contains "Larry and Henry." Unsigned. Illustrated.

BUCKNELL REVIEW: A SCHOLARLY JOURNAL OF LETTERS, ARTS, AND SCIENCES, XI: 2 (March 1963). Contains Charles I. Glicksberg, "The Fictional World of Lawrence Durrell."

CENTENNIAL REVIEW, VII: 2 (Spring 1963). Contains Alfred M. Bork, "Durrell and Relativity."

STUDIES: AN IRISH QUARTERLY REVIEW, LII: 205 (Spring 1963). Contains John C. Kelly, S.J., "Lawrence Durrell: *The Alexandria Quartet*."

REPORTER, XXVII (11 April 1963). Contains David Littlejohn, "What They Wrote and What They Were."

UNIVERSITY OF TORONTO QUARTERLY, XXXII: 3 (April 1963). Contains Herbert Howarth, "A Segment of Durrell's Quartet."

THE SOUTH ATLANTIC QUARTERLY, LXII: 3 (Summer

1963). Contains Gerald Jay Goldberg, "The
Search for the Artist in Some Recent
British Fiction."

STUDIES: AN IRISH QUARTERLY REVIEW, LII: 206
(Summer 1963). Contains John C. Kelly,
S. J., "Lawrence Durrell's Style."

DIETSCHE WARANDE EN BELFOR, CVIII (1963).
Contains Herman Servotte, "The Alexandria
Quartet van Lawrence Durrell."

Gindin, James. *POSTWAR BRITISH FICTION*.
Berkeley, Calif.: University of California
Press, 1962.

---. Berkeley, Calif.: University of California
Press, 1963. Paperback.

Glicksberg, Charles I. *THE SELF IN MODERN
LITERATURE*. University Park: Pennsylvania
State University Press, 1963. Contains
"The Alexandria Quartet."

Hartt, Julian N. *THE LOST IMAGE OF MAN*. Baton
Rouge: Louisiana State University Press,
1963.

Hawkins, Tiger Tim. *EVE: THE COMMON MUSE OF
HENRY MILLER AND LAWRENCE DURRELL*. San
Francisco: The Ahat Press, 1963.

Jennings, Paul. *OODLES OF ODDLIES*. London:
Max Reinhardt, 1963. Contains "East
Bergholt Quartet." ["I read Mr. Lawrence
Durrell's *Alexandria Quartet*, rather
belatedly, at a time when we were looking
after Twemlow, an Abyssinian guinea-pig
belonging to neighbours on holiday. We
have a female cat (Elliott), a neuter
(William Byrd) and a spaniel (Barker)."]

LEXIKON DER WELTLITERATUR. Edited by Gero von Wilpert. Stuttgart: Kroner, 1963. Contains "Lawrence Durrell."

---. Revised edition. 1975.

WRITERS AT WORK: THE PARIS REVIEW INTERVIEWS. Introduced by Van Wyck Brooks. London: Secker and Warburg, 1963. Contains "Lawrence Durrell."

---. New York: Viking, 1963.

ΕΙΚΟΝΕΣ (Athens), No. 404 (19 July 1963). Contains Λώρενς Ντάρρελ, Φίλιππος Σερράρντ (Phillip Sherrard, "Lawrence Durrell"). Illustrated.

CURRENT BIOGRAPHY, XXIV (July 1963). Contains a short biographical sketch of Durrell which subsequently appeared in *Current Biography Yearbook 1963*. Portrait.

DIE WELT (Hamburg) (31 August 1963). Contains Willy Haas, "Salamander, Lemuren, Nachtmare. . . Ein neuer Faust, diesmal aus keltischem Geist."

ENCOUNTER, XXI: 2 (August 1963). Contains D. J. Enright, "Public Faeces," a review of *A Private Correspondence*.

WISCONSIN STUDIES IN CONTEMPORARY LITERATURE, IV: 23 (Autumn 1963). Contains Lee T. Lemon, "*The Alexandria Quartet*: Form and Fiction."

HAMBURGER ABENDBLATT (Hamburg) (14 Dezember 1963). Contains W[alter] M. H[ermann], "Vor der dritten Durrell-Premiere. Im Schauspielhaus: Letzte Proben zum *Irischen Faust*. Der Dichter ist dabei." Photographs of Durrell with the director,

O. F. Schuh and Will Quadflieg (Faust/Dr.
Morienus), and of Durrell with his wife,
Claude, and the German translator of *An
Irish Faustus*, Ursula Schuh.

---. (19 Dezember 1963). Contains Walter M.
Hermann, "Dritte Durrell-Uraufführung im
Schauspielhaus. Fragwürdige Macht über
die Materie. Zwiespältiger *Irischer
Faust*--brilliant inszeniert." With two
photographs from the Hamburg production.

FRANKFURTER ALLGEMEINE ZEITUNG (Frankfurt)
(20 Dezember 1963). Contains Klaus Wagner,
"Höllenfahrt und Gipfelruh. *Ein irischer
Faust* von Lawrence Durrell in Hamburg
uraufgeführt."

DIE WELT (Hamburg) (20 Dezember 1963). Contains
Willy Haas, "Alchimist auf Höllenfahrt.
Lawrence Durrells Drama *Ein irischer Faust*
in Hamburg uraufgeführt."

KURIER (Berlin) (23 Dezember 1963). Contains
Claus Henning Bachmann, "Der neue Durrell
Ein irischer Faust in Hamburg. Alchemie
steht für Kernphysik."

SUEDDEUTSCHE ZEITUNG (München) (23 Dezember
1963). Contains Christa Rotzoll, "Ein
irischer Faust. Durrell-Uraufführung in
Hamburg."

RHEINISCHE MERKUR (Koblenz), No. 52 (1963).
Contains Heinz Beckmann, "Kartenspiel mit
dem Nichts. Durrells irischer Faust wird
Gehilfe eines Ablasskrämers."

DER SPIEGEL (Hamburg), XVII: 52 (25 Dezember
1963). Contains "Larrys Faust," an
article on *An Irish Faustus*, with
photographs of Durrell with the director,

O. F. Schuh, and of Beatrice Norden
(Margret) and Will Quadflieg (Faust/Dr.
Morienus).

BOOKS ABROAD, XXXVII: 1 (Winter 1963). Contains
Herbert Howarth, "Lawrence Durrell and
Some Early Masters."

THE PERSONALIST, XLIV: 1 (Winter 1963).
Contains Nancy Sullivan, "Lawrence
Durrell's Epitaph for the Novel."

DIE VOLKSBUEHNE (Hamburg), XIV (1963-64).
Contains Rolf Wilken, "Zur Uraufführung
von Lawrence Durrells *Ein irischer Faust*."

TELEGRAF (Berlin) (3 Januar 1964). Contains
Alfred Gajewski, "Roter Faden zu dünn.
Durrells *Irischer Faust* uraufgeführt."

TIME (New York), LXXXII (3 January 1964).
Contains "Goethe Go Home," an unsigned
review of *An Irish Faustus*.

TAGESSPIEGEL (Berlin) (4 Januar 1964). Contains
Johannes Jacobi, "Kein Faust—ein Fäustchen
nur. Oscar Fritz Schuh inszeniert Lawrence
Durrells *Ein irischer Faust*."

THE TIMES (London) (7 January 1964). Contains
"Durrell Writes an Irish Pantomime," a
review of *An Irish Faustus*.

REVIEW, IX (January 1964). Contains Peter March,
a review of *New Poems 1963*, which was
edited by Lawrence Durrell.

CRITIQUE: STUDIES IN MODERN FICTION, VII: 1
(Spring 1964). Contains John V. Hagopian,
"The Resolution of *The Alexandria Quartet*."

EDGE (Canada), No. 2 (Spring 1964). Contains

W. F. Smyth, "Lawrence Durrell--Modern
Love in Chamber Pots and Space Time."

ENGLISH RECORD, XIV: 4 (April 1964). Contains
    Peter Cortland, "Durrell's Sentimentalism."

THE SUNDAY TELEGRAPH (London) (12 April 1964).
    Contains "Goodbye Oscar," on the revelation
    that Durrell was Oscar Epfs.

SUEDDEUTSCHE ZEITUNG (München) (30 Mai 1964).
    Contains Barbara Klie, "Durrells Blüten
    von Rhodos."

FRANKFURTER HEFTE (Neuwied) (Juni 1964).
    Contains Henry Miller, "Brief an Lawrence
    Durrell. Big Sur, 10/31/59," a
    prepublication excerpt from *A Private
    Correspondence*.

MODERN FICTION STUDIES, X: 2 (Summer 1964).
    Contains A. K. Weatherhead, "Romantic
    Anachronisms in *The Alexandria Quartet*."

VIRGINIA QUARTERLY REVIEW, XL: 3 (Summer 1964).
    Contains Robert Scholes, "Return to
    Alexandria: Lawrence Durrell and Western
    Narrative Tradition." [Later reprinted
    in *The Fabulators* (1967).]

AMBIT, XIX (1964). Contains Martin C. O. Bax,
    a review of *P. E. N. Anthology: New Poems
    1963*, which was edited by Durrell.

Bronowski, J. *INSIGHT*. London: Macdonald,
    1964. Contains "The Vision of Our Age,"
    part of which is an interview with
    Durrell in which he discusses his
    treatment of space and time in *The
    Alexandria Quartet*.

ON CONTEMPORARY LITERATURE: AN ANTHOLOGY OF

*CRITICAL ESSAYS ON THE MAJOR MOVEMENTS
AND WRITERS OF CONTEMPORARY LITERATURE.*
New York: Avon Books, 1964. Contains John
Unterecker, "The Protean World of Lawrence
Durrell," adapted from his *Lawrence
Durrell* (Columbia University Press, 1964).

Powell, Lawrence Clark. *THE LITTLE PACKAGE:
PAGES ON LITERATURE AND LANDSCAPE FROM A
TRAVELLING BOOKMAN'S LIFE.* Cleveland:
World, 1964. Contains "Durrell in Dallas."

Pritchett, V. S. *THE LIVING NOVEL AND LATER
APPRECIATIONS.* New York: Random House,
1964. Contains "Alexandrian Hothouse."
[Reprinted 1967.]

DER VLAAMSE GIDS, XLVIII (1964). Contains Piet
van Aken, "Open(hartig) Wederwoord aan
PDW."

ΕΙΚΟΝΕΣ (Athens), No. 457 (24 July 1964).
Contains Ἀνάμνηεν καί στόχος (Memories
and Plans). Illustrated.

CONTEMPORARY REVIEW, CCV: 1182 (July 1964).
Contains Beryl Gaster, "Lawrence Durrell."

*MERKUR: DEUTSCHE ZEITSCHRIFT FUR EUROPAISCHES
DENKEN*, XVIII: 7 (July 1964). Contains
Reinhard Baumgard, "Rückblickend von vorn
gesehen: Lawrence Durrell."

DUBLINER, III: 3 (Autumn 1964). Contains
Deborah De Vere White, a review of *Selected
Poems, 1935-1963.*

THE DAILY EXPRESS (London) (8 December 1964).
Contains Ann Leslie, "The Master's Choice:
This Infuriating Man," an interview with
Durrell about French Writer Claude
Seignolle. Illustrated.

OUTPOSTS, LXIII (Winter 1964). Contains Hugh
     Creighton Hill, a review of *Selected Poems,
     1935-1963.*

MODERN FICTION STUDIES, X: 4 (Winter 1964-65).
     Contains H. Dare, "The Quest for Durrell's
     Scobie."

IRISH DIGEST, LXXXII (February 1965). Contains
     Ann Leslie, "This Infuriating Man--Lawrence
     Durrell." [Reprinted from *The Daily Express*
     (8 December 1964).]

ΤΗΛΕΓΡΑΦΟΣ [*Telegraph*] (Corfu) (25 May 1965).
     Contains Πηγή ἐμπνεύσεως ἡ Κέρκυρα γιά
     τόν Ντάρρελ (Corfu is a Well of Inspiration
     for Durrell). Illustrated.

THE DAILY TELEGRAPH (London) (13 June 1965).
     Contains "Sunday Morning with Mandrake:
     Durrell Favourite for the Nobel?"

REVUE DE PARIS (Juin 1965). Contains R. M.
     Alberes, "Lawrence Durrell ou le Roman
     Pentagonal."

CONTEMPORARY BRITISH NOVELISTS. Edited by Karl
     Shapiro. Carbondale: Southern Illinois
     University Press, 1965. Contains Louis
     Fraiberg, "Durrell's Dissonant Quartet."

ECRIVAINS CONTEMPORAINS. Paris: Editions d'Art
     Lucien Mazenod, 1965. Contains a page
     about Durrell by F.-J. Temple. Colored
     photograph.

*INSIGHT II: ANALYSES OF MODERN BRITISH
     LITERATURE.* Edited by John V. Hagopian
     and Martin Dolch. Frankfurt: Hirschgraben-
     Verlag, 1965. Contains John V. Hagopian,
     "Lawrence Durrell: The Halcyon Summer."

KINDLER LITERATUR LEXIKON. Zürich: Kindler,
     1965. Contains Gertrud Baruch, *"The
     Alexandria Quartet*." [Includes a selected
     bibliography.]

DER MODERNE ENGLISCHE ROMAN: INTERPRETATIONEN.
     Edited by Horst Oppel. Berlin: Erich
     Schmidt Verlag, 1965. Contains Robert
     Fricker, "Lawrence Durrell: The Alexandria
     Quartet." [Reprinted 1971.]

LA NACION (1965). Contains Miguel Alfred
     Olivera, "La Trayectoria de un Fugaz
     Cometa: Lawrence Durrell," a rare
     recollection of someone who knew Durrell
     during his stay in Argentina. Moreover,
     the article also mentions that the first
     performance of *Sappho* was given at Yale
     University (not Hamburg as is generally
     believed), after which the text was
     considerably altered before the Hamburg
     premiere.

Rippier, Joseph S. *SOME POSTWAR BRITISH
     NOVELISTS*. Frankfurt: Verlag Moritz
     Diesterweg, 1965.

Weigel, John A. *LAWRENCE DURRELL*. New York:
     Twayne, 1965.

———. New York: E. P. Dutton, 1966. Paperback.

Widmer, Kingsley. *THE LITERARY REBEL*.
     Carbondale: Southern Illinois University
     Press, 1965.

YALE FRENCH STUDIES, No. 35 (1965). Contains
     Joseph J. McMahon, "Where does Real Life
     begin?"

REFLETS MEDITERRANEENS (Avignon) (Juin-Juillet
     1965). Contains R. Allan, "Entretien avec

Lawrence Durrell," and F.-J. Temple, "Lawrence Durrell, l'Homme et l'Oeuvre."

COLORADO QUARTERLY, XIV: 1 (Summer 1965). Contains David Littlejohn, "The Permanence of Durrell."

CHRIST UND WELT (Stuttgart), No. 45 (1965). Contains Ingrid Parigi, "Eine Frau aus England. Lawrence Durrell und die Päpstin Johanna."

ΚΕΡΚΥΡΑΙΚΑ ΝΕΑ [*Corfu News*] (17 January 1966). Contains Ἡ Κέρκυρα ὅπως τὴν εἶδε Χένρυ Μύλλερ. Ὁ Ἀμερικανόσ που τή γνώριδε μαζύ μέ τόν Ντάρρελ [Corfu as seen by Henry Miller: the American who knew the Island as the guest of Durrell].

LONDON MAGAZINE, V: 12 (March 1966). Contains Robin Fedden, "Personal Landscape."

CRITIQUE, VIII (Spring 1966). Contains Ann Gossman, "Some Characters in Search of a Mirror."

LA NOUVELLE REVUE FRANCAISE (Paris), 14e anneé, No. 162 (Juin 1966). Contains Alain Bosquet, "Lawrence Durrell ou l'Azur Ironique."

BALCONY, No. 5 (1966). Contains Ron Howard, "The Plays of Lawrence Durrell."

DRAMA STUDIES, V (1966). Contains Douglas Cole, "Faust and Anti-Faust in Modern Drama."

Enright, D[ennis] J[oseph]. *CONSPIRATORS AND POETS*. London: Chatto & Windus, 1966. Contains "Alexandrian Night's Entertainment: Durrell's Quartet" and "Public Faeces: The Correspondence of Lawrence Durrell and Henry Miller."

Fedden, Robin. *PERSONAL LANDSCAPE*. London:
Turret Books, 1966. An account of the
genesis of the magazine *Personal Landscape*.
(See Section E.) [Limited to 1,000 copies,
the first 50 numbered and signed by the
author. Two illustrations. Limited
edition bound in cloth, ordinary edition
in paper wrappers. A portion of this
book appeared in *The London Magazine*,
V: 12 (March 1966).]

Fricker, Robert. *DER MODERNE ENGLISCHE ROMAN*.
Göttingen: Vandenhoeck und Ruprecht, 1966.
Contains "Lawrence Durrell."

HORISONT, XIII: 2 (1966). Contains Sture
Hagergard, "Om Medvetandets Struktur."

NIVEL, XLIV (1966). Contains Fernando Sanchez
Mayans, "Miller y Durrell publican Su
Correspondencia."

Stephanides, Theodore. *THE GOLDEN FACE: POEMS*.
London: The Fortune Press, 1965 [1966].
Contains "The Submerged Garden (Kassopi,
Corfu, 1939)," with reference in the notes
to Lawrence Durrell. [Dr. Stephanides is
one of the leading figures in *Prospero's
Cell*.]

DIE WELT (Hamburg) (7 Juli 1966). Contains Anne
Uhde, "Kein Räuberpistole. Ein neuer
Durrell. Lawrence Durrell: *Weisse Adler
über Serbien*."

BEAUX-ARTS (Brussels), No. 1145 (3 Decembre
1966). Contains F.-J. Temple, "Lawrence
Durrell Dix Ans Après." Contains
photograph of Durrell, Temple, and Miller.

THE QUEEN (7 December 1966). Contains Peter
Carvell, "Why Doesn't Mr. Durrell Write
To Me?"

*SHENANDOAH: THE WASHINGTON AND LEE UNIVERSITY
     REVIEW*, XVIII: 4 (Summer 1967). Contains
     W. R. Robinson, "Intellect and Imagination
     in *The Alexandria Quartet*."

*ENGLISH MISCELLANY: A SYMPOSIUM OF HISTORY,
     LITERATURE AND THE ARTS*, XVIII. Edited by
     Mario Praz. Rome: Longmans, for The
     British Council, 1967. Contains Giuseppe
     Sertoli, "Lawrence Durrell e il 'Quartetto
     di Alessandria.'"

Levine, David. *PENS AND NEEDLES: LITERARY
     CARICATURES*. Selected and introduced by
     John Updike. Boston: Gambit, 1967.
     Contains a caricature of Durrell.

---. London: Andre Deutsch, 1970.

Nin, Anaïs. *THE DIARY OF ANAIS NIN, 1934-1939*.
     New York: The Swallow Press and Harcourt,
     Brace & World, 1967. Contains numerous
     references to Durrell and a 1937 photograph.

Pongs, Hermann. *DAS KLEINE LEXIKON DER
     WELTLITERATUR*. Stuttgart: Union-Verlag,
     1967. Contains "Lawrence Durrell."

DER SCHAUSPIELFUEHRER, Band 8. Edited by
     Joseph Gregor. Stuttgart: Hiersemann,
     1967. Contains Siegfried Kienzle,
     "*Sappho*."

Scholes, Robert. *THE FABULATORS*. New York:
     Oxford University Press, 1967. Contains
     "Lawrence Durrell and The Return to
     Alexandria."

Sertoli, Giuseppe. *LAWRENCE DURRELL*. Milan:
     U. Mersia & Co., 1967.

Steiner, George. *LANGUAGE AND SILENCE: ESSAYS*

ON LANGUAGE, LITERATURE, AND THE INHUMAN.
New York: Atheneum, 1967. Contains
"Lawrence Durrell and The Baroque Novel,"
reprinted from *Yale Review*, XLIX: 4
(June 1960).

MODERN FICTION STUDIES: LAWRENCE DURRELL SPECIAL
NUMBER, XIII: 3 (Autumn 1967). Contains
critical essays by nine hands.

DIE WELT (Hamburg) (12 Oktober 1967). Contains
Ulrich Schapauff, "Ozean in der Feder.
Zum Briefwechsel L. Durrell--H. Miller."

WISCONSIN STUDIES IN CONTEMPORARY LITERATURE,
VIII (Winter 1967). Contains Alan Warren
Friedman, "Key to Lawrence Durrell."

THE DAILY EXPRESS (London) (13 February 1968).
Contains Peter Grosvenor, "Wine. . . sun
. . .women: What Best-Sellers have done
for Lawrence Durrell." Illustrated.

JUPITER AND TURRET AT THE WIGMORE: NEW JAZZ AND
MODERN POETRY (15 February 1968). [The
program includes "In Arcadia" and "Lesbos,"
which were set to music by Wallace Southam.]

DER SPIEGEL (Hamburg), No. 6 (Februar 1968).
Contains Siegfried Lenz, "Uber Lawrence
Durrell/Henry Miller *Briefe.* Von Genie
zu Genie."

ISIS (Oxford), No. 1552 (21 February 1968).
Contains Philip Hodson, "Lawrence Durrell
and His Poetry."

BRITISH MEDICAL JOURNAL (9 March 1968). Contains
the letter by Chong Tong Mun cited in
Nunquam.

THE SUNDAY TIMES (London) (7 April 1968).

Contains Anthony Burgess, "Durrell's
Seraglio," a review of *Tunc*.

THE LISTENER (London) (11 April 1968). Contains
D. J. Enright, "More and More Mysterious,"
a review of *Tunc*.

THE NEW YORK TIMES BOOK REVIEW, LXXIII: 15
(14 April 1968). Contains Peter Collier,
"A Talk with Lawrence Durrell" (an
interview at Henry Miller's home in
California), and Gerald Sykes, "Durrell's
1984," a review of *Tunc*.

PUBLISHERS' WEEKLY: THE BOOK INDUSTRY JOURNAL,
CXCII: 17 (22 April 1968). Contains
"Authors and Editors."

THE SUNDAY EXPRESS (London) (28 April 1968).
Contains Robert Pitman, "Has Mr. Durrell
Cast his Strange Spell over You?"

BOOKS AND BOOKMEN (London), XIII: 4 (April 1968).
Contains Bolivar Le Franc, "A Very
Optimistic Man," an interview about *Tunc*.

SATURDAY REVIEW, LI: 18 (4 May 1968). Contains
Robert J. Clements, "European Literary
Scene," which contains a note on the
P. E. N. Club reception for Durrell at the
Hotel Pierre.

DURHAM UNIVERSITY JOURNAL, n.s. XXIX: 3 (June
1968). Contains Jean Hamard, "Lawrence
Durrell: A European Writer."

BROCKHAUS ENZYKLOPAEDIE IN 20 BAENDEN, Band 5.
Wiesbaden: Brockhaus, 1968. Contains
"Lawrence Durrell."

COLLECTED ESSAYS BY MEMBERS OF THE FACULTY,
No. 11. Kyoritsu, Japan: Kyoritsu

Women's Junior College, 1968. Contains
Masako Kameyama, "Lawrence Durrell: A
Sketch."

Fraser, G. S. *LAWRENCE DURRELL: A STUDY*. With
a Bibliography by Alan G. Thomas. London:
Faber & Faber, 1968.

---. Revised edition. 1973.

LEXIKON DER WELTLITERATUR, II: *WERKE*. Edited by
Gero von Wilpert. Stuttgart: Kröner, 1968.
Contains Horst Drescher on *The Alexandria
Quartet*, and Siegfried Kienzle on *Sappho*
and *Acte*.

---. Revised edition. 1980. This edition adds
Wilhelm Gauger's comments on *Tunc*, *Nunquam*,
Monsieur, and *Livia*.

Press, John. *THE CHEQUER'D SHADE: REFLECTIONS
ON OBSCURITY IN POETRY*. London: Oxford
University Press, 1968. Contains
quotations from and a discussion of
"Cities, Plains and People," "Five
Soliloquies," "A Private Country," and
Key to Modern British Poetry.

REVUE DES LANGUES VIVANTES, XXIV: 2 (1968).
Contains Roland Decanq, "What Lies Beyond:
An Analysis of Darley's 'Quest' in
Lawrence Durrell's *Alexandria Quartet*."

SECOLUL, XX: 9 (1968). Contains Simona Draghici,
"Geneza unei Tetralogi," and Mihai Cornel
Ionescu, "Alexandria: *Eros*, *Agape*, *Agon*."

WRITING IN ENGLAND TODAY: THE LAST FIFTEEN YEARS.
Edited by Karl Miller. Harmondsworth,
Middlesex: Penguin Books, 1968. Contains
D. J. Enright, "Alexandrian Night's
Entertainment."

---. Baltimore, Md.: Penguin Books, 1968.

NEW YORK REVIEW, XI: 1 (11 July 1968). Contains
     Bernard Bergonzi, "Stale Incense."

TWENTIETH CENTURY LITERATURE, XIV: 2 (July 1968).
     Contains John A. Weigel, "Lawrence
     Durrell's First Novel."

THE DAILY TELEGRAPH (London) (8 August 1968).
     Contains Martin Green, "Lawrence Durrell's
     Self-Made Myth," a review of G. S. Fraser,
     Lawrence Durrell: A Study.

THE NEW STATESMAN (London), No. 76 (2 August
     1968). Contains Francis Hope, "Olives and
     After," a review of G. S. Fraser, *Lawrence
     Durrell: A Study*.

DIE WELT (Hamburg) (29 September 1968). Contains
     Carl Brinitzer, "Wenn Diplomaten aus der
     Schule plaudern. . . Lawrence Durrell:
     Esprit de Corps."

FRANKFURTER ALLGEMEINE ZEITUNG (Frankfurt)
     (30 November 1968). Contains Günter
     Blöcker, "Kavernen des schwarzen Humors.
     Erzählungen von Lawrence Durrell.
     Lawrence Durrell: *Esprit de Corps*."

*CALIBAN: ANNALES DE LA FACULTE DES LETTRES DE
     TOULOUSE*, VI: Tome V/1 (Janvier 1969).
     Contains Gérard Lebas, "La Critique et le
     Quatuor d'Alexandrie." [A useful
     supplement to this volume.]

THE DAILY MAIL (London) (27 February 1969).
     Contains a report by Denis Holmes on the
     film "Justine," including comments by
     Durrell. Illustrated.

TRAVEL AND CAMERA: THE INTERNATIONAL MAGAZINE

OF TRAVEL AND PHOTOGRAPHY, XXXII: 3
(March 1969). Contains "Brassaï's Paris,"
which quotes Durrell.

COMPARATIVE LITERATURE, XXI (Spring 1969).
Contains C. Katope, "Cavafy and Durrell's
The Alexandria Quartet."

SATURDAY REVIEW, LII (14 June 1969). Contains
John Unterecker, "Art as Intersecting
Fields of Energy," a review of *Spirit of
Place*.

NEW REPUBLIC, CLX: 25 (21 June 1969). Contains
George Wickes, "Durrell's Landscapes," a
review of *Spirit of Place*.

Durrell, Gerald. *BIRDS, BEASTS AND RELATIVES*.
London: Collins, 1969. [A companion
volume to *My Family and Other Animals*.]

---. New York: Viking, 1969.

FILOLOGIA MODERNA, XXXVII (1969). Contains
Micaela Misiego, "Lawrence Durrell y su
Alexandria Quartet."

Isernhagen, Hartwig. *SENSATION, VISION AND
IMAGINATION: THE PROBLEM OF UNITY IN
DURRELL'S NOVELS*. Bamberg: Rodenbusch,
1969.

Press, John. *A MAP OF MODERN ENGLISH VERSE*.
London: Oxford University Press, 1969.
[Durrell is discussed briefly in the
chapter "Poets of the Second World War
and of the 1940s."]

BOOK-COLLECTING AND LIBRARY MONTHLY (Brighton),
No. 15 (July 1969). Contains John
Gawsworth, "My Friend Lawrence Durrell,"
and B. Hutchinson, a notice of *Spirit of
Place*.

NATION, CCIX: 2 (14 July 1969). Contains Joan
   Goulianos, "Landscape of the Heart," a
   review of *Spirit of Place*.

BOOK-COLLECTING AND LIBRARY MONTHLY (Brighton),
   No. 16 (August 1969). Contains John
   Gawsworth, "Somewhat of Lawrence Durrell."

MINAS GERAIS: SUPLEMENTO LITERARIO (13 September
   1969). Contains Luis Gonzaga Vieira,
   "Pursewarden."

SUEDDEUTSCHE ZEITUNG (München) (27 September
   1969). Contains K. H. Kramberg, "Damals
   in Athen. Lawrence Durrell: *Tunc*."

MADEMOISELLE, LXIX (September 1969). Contains
   Julie Burns, "Art is Very Curative. . .
   You Purge Yourself by Putting Down: An
   Interview with Lawrence Durrell."

FRANKFURTER RUNDSCHAU (Frankfurt) (10 Oktober
   1969). Contains Günter Blöcker, "Uber
   alle Wirklichkeit hinaus. *Tunc*--nach
   langem Schweigen ein neuer Roman von
   Lawrence Durrell."

TAGESSPIEGEL (Berlin) (19 Oktober 1969).
   Contains Otto F. Beer, "Ein geheimnisvolles
   Teppichmuster. Lawrence Durrell: *Tunc*."

DIE WELT (Hamburg) (23 Oktober 1969). Contains
   Christian Ferber, "Alexandrinische
   Liebesgeschichte, in Gold gefasst.
   Lawrence Durrell: *Tunc*."

THE VIRGINIA QUARTERLY REVIEW, XLV: 4 (Autumn
   1969). Contains Joan Goulianos, "Lawrence
   Durrell and Alexandria."

PRAIRIE SCHOONER, XLIV [i.e., XLIII]: 4 (Winter
   1969-70). Contains John Paul Russo,

"Love in Lawrence Durrell."

THE DAILY SKETCH (London) (6 March 1970).
Contains "Mr. Durrell, signing in."

SATURDAY REVIEW (21 March 1970). Contains
Anthony Burgess, "Durrell and the
Homunculi," an extended review of *Nunquam*.

THE GUARDIAN (Manchester) (23 March 1970).
Contains Terry Coleman, "Mocker of the
Spare Parts Age: Lawrence Durrell—He
Believes We Are Now at a Point of Now
or Never." Illustrated.

THE TIMES LITERARY SUPPLEMENT (London),
No. 3,552 (26 March 1970). Contains "The
Long Arm of the Firm," an unsigned review
of *Nunquam*.

THE SPECTATOR (London) (28 March 1970).
Contains Trevor Grove, "Now and Then," a
review of *Nunquam*.

THE NEW YORK TIMES BOOK REVIEW (29 March 1970).
Contains Richard Boston, a review of
Nunquam.

THE SUNDAY TIMES (London) (29 March 1970).
Contains Julian Jebb, "Boom and Treacle,"
a review of *Nunquam*.

STEAUA, XXI: 4 (April 1970). Contains Virgil
Stanciu, "Lawrence Durrell—Un Profil."

THE SUNDAY TIMES (London) (10 May 1970).
Contains Michael Bateman, "Concerning
Ulysses, Sketch for a Musical by Lawrence
Durrell," with humorous illustrations by
Ralph Steadman.

TIME (New York), XCV (18 May 1970). Contains
an unsigned review of *Nunquam*.

NOUSE (York), No. 56 (28 May 1970). This issue of the York University Newspaper contains "Spotlight: Osric Allen talks to Lawrence Durrell." Illustrated.

CHICAGO SUN TIMES (12 June 1970[?]). Contains Colman Andrews, "Showcase: Durrell Brings a Catchy Muse to Ulysses' Lusty Adventures." Illustrated.

Aldington, Richard. *SELECTED CRITICAL WRITINGS, 1928-1960*. Edited by Alister Kershaw, with a Preface by Harry T. Moore. Carbondale: Southern Illinois University Press, 1970. Contains "Lawrence Durrell," reprinted from *Two Cities* (1959).

ANALELE UNIVERSITATI BUCURESTI. LIMBI GERMANICE. (1970). Contains Domnica Bottea, "Structura, Timp si Spatiu in Tetralogia lui Lawrence Durrell."

CALIBAN: ANNALES DE LA FACULTE DES LETTRES ET HUMAINES DE TOULOUSE, VII: Tome VI/1 (1970). Contains Gérard Lebas, "Le Mecanisme de l'Espace-Temps dans le *Quatuor*."

ENGLISCHE LITERATUR DER GEGENWART. Edited by Horst W. Drescher. Stuttgart: Kröner, 1970. Contains Wiklef Hoops, "Lawrence Durrell."

Fielding, Daphne. *THE NEAREST WAY HOME*. London: Eyre & Spottiswoode, 1970. This book by the wife of Xan Fielding contains several references to Durrell and Claude, as well as two photographs taken at their mazet near Nimes.

Fraser, G. S. *WRITERS AND THEIR WORK*, No. 216: *LAWRENCE DURRELL*. London: The Longman Group for The British Council, 1970.

Friedman, Alan Warren. *ART FOR LOVE'S SAKE: LAWRENCE DURRELL AND THE ALEXANDRIA QUARTET.* Norman: University of Oklahoma Press, 1970. Includes a letter by Durrell and a Bibliography.

THE NEW YORK REVIEW (23 July 1970). Contains Christopher Ricks, "Female and Other Impersonators."

ART INTERNATIONAL, XIV (September 1970). Contains R. C. Kennedy, "Lawrence Durrell: *Tunc-Nunquam*."

DIE WELT (Hamburg) (19 Oktober 1970). Contains "Das Geheimnis des Malers Epfs lüftet Durrell jetzt in Paris." With a photograph of Durrell carrying two paintings.

DIE ZEIT (Hamburg), No. 47 (1970). Contains Otto F. Beer, "Elektronische Mythologie in Lawrence Durrells *Tunc* und *Nunquam*."

ORIZONT, XXII: 1 (January 1971). Contains Adina Arsenescu, "Durrell si Lumea sa Complexa."

TAGESSPIEGEL (Berlin) (7 Marz 1971). Contains Otto F. Beer, "Frankenstein im elektronischen Zeitalter. Lawrence Durrells *Nunquam*."

JOURNAL OF MODERN LITERATURE, I: 3 (March 1971). Contains William Leigh Godshalk, "Aspects of Lawrence Durrell," a review of *Spirit of Place*, G. S. Fraser's *Lawrence Durrell: A Study*, and Alan Warren Friedman's *Art for Love's Sake: Lawrence Durrell and The Alexandria Quartet*.

DIE NEUEREN SPRACHEN (Frankfurt/Bonn), n.s. XX: 6 (Juni 1971). Contains Horst W. Drescher, "Raumzeit: Zur Struktur von Lawrence

Durrells *Alexandria Quartet*;" Johannes
Gottwald, "Der Kunstlerroman Darleys:
Kontinuitat in Lawrence Durrells
Alexandria Quartet," and Leo Truchlar,
"Versuch über Lawrence Durrell."

MODERN FICTION STUDIES, XVII: 2 (Summer 1971).
Contains Joan Rodman Goulianos, "A
Conversation with Lawrence Durrell about
Art, Analysis, and Politics," and Chet
Taylor, "Dissonance and Digression: The
Ill-Fitting Fusion of Philosophy and Form
in Lawrence Durrell's *Alexandria Quartet*."

*CALIBAN: ANNALES DE LA FACULTE DES LETTRES ET
HUMAINES DE TOULOUSE*, VIII: Tome VII/1
(1971). Contains Gérard Lebas, "The
Fabric of Durrell's *Alexandria Quartet*."

CRITIQUE, XIII: 2 (1971). Contains Ann Gossman,
"Love's Alchemy in *The Alexandria Quartet*."

Durrell, Gerald. *FILLETS OF PLAICE*. London:
Collins, 1971. [A companion to *Birds,
Beasts and Relatives* and *My Family and
Other Animals*.]

---. New York: Viking, 1971.

Greene, Graham. *A SORT OF LIFE*. London: Bodley
Head, 1971. Contains "Discrimination in
one's words is certainly required, but not
love of one's words--that is a form of
self-love, a fatal love which leads a
young writer to the excesses of Charles
Morgan and Lawrence Durrell, and looking
back at this period of my life, I can see
I was in danger of taking their road. I
was only saved by failure."

Lennartz, Franz. *AUSLAENDISCHE DICHTER UND
SCHRIFTSTELLER UNSERER ZEIT*. Stuttgart:
Kröner, 1971. Contains "Lawrence Durrell."

With a selected bibliography.

LEXIKON 2000: GROSSE FARBIGE ENZYKLOPADIE IN 12 BANDEN, IV. Stuttgart: Wissen-Verlag, 1971. Contains "Lawrence Durrell."

Neuhaus, Volker. *LITERATUR UND LEBEN*, n.s. XIII: *TYPEN MULTIPERSPEKTIVISCHEN ERZAEHLENS*. Köln, Wien: Böhlau, 1971. Contains "*The Alexandria Quartet*."

Olles, Helmut, ed. *LITERATURLEXIKON DES 20. JAHRHUNDERTS*. Hamburg: Rowholt Verlag, 1971. Contains Helmut Olles, "Lawrence Durrell."

Steiner, Gerhard, ed. *FREMDSPRACHIGE SCHRIFTSTELLER*. Leipzig: Bibliographisches Institut, 1971. Contains "Lawrence Durrell."

———. 1977. Contains Georg Seehase, "Lawrence Durrell."

Tarpley, Fred, and Ann Moseley, eds. *OF EDSELS AND MARAUDERS*. Commerce, Texas: Names Institute Press, 1971. Contains "Charactonyms in *The Alexandria Quartet*: Threads in a Tapestry."

SEMNELE ROMANULUI. Bucharest: Cartea Romaneasca, 1971. Contains Ion Vitner, "Lawrence Durrell si romanul poliedric."

SHENANDOAH: THE WASHINGTON AND LEE UNIVERSITY REVIEW, XXII: 2 (Winter 1971). Contains Eugene Lyons and Harry T. Antrim, "An Interview with Lawrence Durrell."

LOS ANGELES FREE PRESS, IX: 2 (January 1972). Contains "Lawrence Durrell on Henry Miller: Registering the Orgasm in One's

Soul," an interview with Durrell about
Miller.

NOTES ON LITERATURE, No. 126 (January 1972).
Contains G. S. Fraser, a note on Durrell's
poetry.

*INTERPRESS: INTERNATIONALER BIOGRAPHISCHER
PRESSEDIENST*. (Hamburg) (15 Februar
1972). Contains "Durrell, Lawrence.
England. Der britische Schriftsteller
Lawrence Durrell wird am 27. Februar
60."

FRANKFURTER ALLGEMEINE ZEITUNG. (Frankfurt)
(26 Februar 1972). Contains "Mittel-
meerische Welt. Lawrence Durrell wird
60."

TAGESSPIEGEL (Berlin) (27 Februar 1972).
Contains "Lawrence Durrell 60."

LONDON MAGAZINE, XII: 1 (April-May 1972).
Contains Herbert Howarth, "Durrell
Snapped in a Library."

Alyn, Marc. *LE GRAND SUPPOSITOIRE: ENTRETIENS
AVEC LAWRENCE DURRELL*. Paris: Pierre
Belfond, 1972. [See Section A.50a.]

---.   London: Abelard-Schuman, 1973.
Translated by Francine Barker.

---.   New York: Grove Press, 1974. Translated
by Francine Barker.

Doyle, Esther M., ed. *STUDIES IN INTERPRETATION*.
Amsterdam: Rodopi, 1972. Contains Joanna
Hawkins Maclay, "The Interpreter and
Modern Fiction: Problems of Point of
View and Structural Tensiveness."

HASIFRUT: QUARTERLY FOR THE STUDY OF LITERATURE, III (1972). Contains Joseph Dan, "Haquadrilogia Ha-Alexandronit shel Lawrence Durrell."

LITERATUR IN WISSENSCHAFT UND UNTERRICHT, V: 2. Kiel: [n.p.,] 1972. Contains Leo Truchlar, "Landschaft des Ich: Kosmo- und Psychogeographie in Lawrence Durrells Reisebüchern."

METHUEN'S STUDY-AID SERIES: GERALD DURRELL'S MY FAMILY AND OTHER ANIMALS. London: Methuen Educational Ltd., 1972. [Contains the obligatory references to 'Brother Larry'.]

Morris, Robert K. *CONTINUANCE AND CHANGE: THE CONTEMPORARY BRITISH NOVEL SEQUENCE*. Carbondale: Southern Illinois University Press, 1972. Contains "Lawrence Durrell, *The Alexandria Quartet*: Art and the Changing Vision."

ORIZONT, XXIII: 2 (1972). Contains Andrei A. Lillin, "Tema cu variatii de prin milenii, vesnic actuala."

OSMANIA JOURNAL OF ENGLISH STUDIES, IX: 1 (1972). Contains Bala Kothandaraman, "The Comic Dimension in *The Alexandria Quartet*."

Rubrecht, Walter Hermann. *SWISS STUDIES IN ENGLISH*, LXXII: *DURRELLS ALEXANDRIA QUARTET: STRUKTUR ALS BEZUGSSYSTEM. SICHTUNG UND ANALYSE*. Berne: Francke Verlag, 1972.

TWENTIETH CENTURY LITERATURE, XVIII: 3 (July 1972). Contains W. Wedin, "The Artist as Narrator in *The Alexandria Quartet*."

CENTENNIAL REVIEW, XVI: 4 (Fall 1972). Contains
R. T. Chapman, "Dead, or Just Pretending?
Reality in *The Alexandria Quartet*."

STUDIES IN THE TWENTIETH CENTURY (Fall 1972).
Contains Edward A. Kopper, "A Note on
the Religious Imagery in *The Alexandria
Quartet*."

OBSERVER MAGAZINE (London) (18 March 1973).
Contains Ruth Hall, "Lawrence Durrell's
First Fling." With two photographs of
Durrell.

KUNST EN CULTUUR, XIX (April 1973). Contains
Mechtilt Meijer Greiner, "Ontmoeting met
Lawrence Durrell."

*ARCADIA: ZEITSCHRIFT FUR VERGLEICHENDE
LITERATURWISSENSCHAFT*, VIII: 1 (1973).
Contains Hartwig Isernhagen, "Die Hähne
Attikas: Lawrence Durrell und Wolfgang
Hildesheimer.:

Drescher, Horst W., and Bernd Kahrmann. *THE
CONTEMPORARY ENGLISH NOVEL: AN ANNOTATED
BIBLIOGRAPHY OF SECONDARY SOURCES*.
Frankfurt: Athenäum Verlag, 1973.
Contains "Lawrence Durrell," which lists
primarily English language studies on
Durrell.

ENGLISH LITERATURE AND LANGUAGE, X (1973).
Contains Mie Kakigahara, "Alexandrie
Shijnso' no Kozo."

Capone, Giovanni. *SPAZA DELLA SCENE COMICA
NELLA NARRATIVE INGLESE*. Pisa:
Goliardica, 1973. Contains a chapter on
Durrell.

MEYERS ENZYKLOPAEDISCHES LEXIKON IN 25 BAENDEN,

VII. Mannheim: Bibliographisches
Institut, Lexikon Verlag, 1973. Contains
"Lawrence Durrell."

MOSAIC (Winnipeg, Man.), VI: 2 (1973). Contains
Walter G. Creed, "Pieces of the Puzzle:
The Multiple-Narrative Structure of *The
Alexandria Quartet.*"

Temple, F.-J., ed. *ENTRETIENS*, XXXII: *LAWRENCE
DURRELL.* Rodez: Editions Subervie, 1973.
Contains personal reminiscences by Miller,
Diana Menuhin, Alfred Perlès, and others;
two poems, by Edward Lucie-Smith and
Christopher Logue, dedicated to Durrell;
critical articles by Gwin Williams,
Edwin Mullins, Richard Aldington, Arthur
Guirdham, and others; the opening section
of *Monsieur, or The Prince of Darkness,*
unedited, in French; and a bibliography.

ICARBS (Southern Illinois University), I: 1
(Fall-Winter 1973). Contains Ian S.
MacNiven, "The Lawrence Durrell
Collection: A Preliminary Examination."
Illustrated.

FAR WESTERN FORUM, I (February 1974). Contains
Carl Dawson, "From Einstein to Keats: A
New Look at *The Alexandria Quartet.*"

LE FIGARO (Paris) (27 Avril 1974). Contains
Guy Le Clec'h, "Durrell adapte. . . et
adopte la papesse Jeanne," an interview
resulting from the publication of the
French translation of *Pope Joan* by
Buchet-Chastel. Illustrated.

TIME (New York) (20 May 1974). Contains a note
and a photograph in "People" on Durrell's
visiting Henry Miller while the latter
recovers from surgery.

Lampert, Gunther. *SYMBOLIK UND LEITMOTIVIK IN LAWRENCE DURRELLS ALEXANDRIA QUARTET*. Bamberg: Rodenbusch, 1974.

BOOKS AND BOOKMEN (London), XIX: 10 (July 1974). Contains Bernard Jones, "World beyond Laughter," a review of *The Revolt of Aphrodite*.

THE OBSERVER (London) (13 October 1974). Contains Anthony Thwaite, "A Matter of Money," a review of *Monsieur, or The Prince of Darkness*.

THE SUNDAY TELEGRAPH (London) (13 October 1974). Contains Francis King, "Alexandrian Maze," a review of *Monsieur, or The Prince of Darkness*.

THE SUNDAY TIMES (London) (13 October 1974). Contains Ronald Blythe, "Cries in the Wilderness," a review of (among others) *Monsieur, or The Prince of Darkness*.

THE DAILY TELEGRAPH (London) (17 October 1974). Contains Tim Heald, "Recent Fiction," a review of *Monsieur, or The Prince of Darkness*.

THE GUARDIAN (Manchester) (17 October 1974). Contains Christopher Wordsworth, "Lampreys on a lordly dish," a review of (among others) *Monsieur, or The Prince of Darkness*.

---.   (18 October 1974). Contains Hugh Hebert, "His Books are Particularly Successful with Women Readers." Portrait.

THE TIMES LITERARY SUPPLEMENT (London), No. 3,789 (18 October 1974). Contains "Devil's Disciples," an unsigned review of *Monsieur, or The Prince of Darkness.*

THE SPECTATOR (London), No. 7,634 (19 October 1974). Contains Peter Ackroyd, "The lower depths," a review of *Monsieur, or The Prince of Darkness.*

AMERICAN LIBRARIES, V: 9 (October 1974). Contains Sheridan Baker, "Alive & Well; The Contemporary British Novel," with a photograph of and an uncomplimentary paragraph about Durrell.

THE IRISH PRESS (23 November 1974). Contains "Novel Notes," which includes a short review of *Monsieur, or The Prince of Darkness.*

TIME (New York) (27 January 1975). Contains John Skow, "Infernal Triangle," a review of *Monsieur, or The Prince of Darkness.*

THE LITERARY GUILD (February 1975). Contains a note on the selection of *Monsieur, or The Prince of Darkness* by the Guild, and a photograph of Durrell.

VIRGINIA WOOLF QUARTERLY, II: 1-2 (Winter-Spring 1975). Contains Suzanne Henig, "Lawrence Durrell: The Greatest of Them All," an interview.

UNDER THE SIGN OF PISCES: ANAIS NIN AND HER CIRCLE (Ohio State University), VI: 2 (Spring 1975). Edited by Richard R. Centing. A special issue on Durrell 'compiled by Brooke Whiting, Department of Special Collections, Research Library, University of California, Los Angeles.' Contains a "Register to the Lawrence Durrell Collection of Manuscript Material" in that Department; "Fragments

of Conversation between Lawrence Durrell,
Henry Miller, and others;" "Lawrence
Durrell at CalTech: An Interview by
Digby Diehl," and some unrelated items.
Also contains a photograph of Durrell,
Miller, and others.

THE LITERARY GUILD (April 1975). Contains a
short interview, "A Quintet for Durrell,"
in which he discusses *Monsieur* and his
plans for the four novels to follow.

ETUDES ANGLAISES, XXVIII: 2 (April–June 1975).
Contains Walter G. Creed, "'The Whole
Pointless Joke'? Darley's Search for
Truth in *The Alexandria Quartet*."

ANTIQUARIAN BOOK MONTHLY REVIEW (Oxford), II: 6
(June 1975). Contains James A. Brigham,
"In Pursuit of Mr. Durrell."

Brassaï. *HENRY MILLER: GRANDEUR NATURE*. Paris:
Gallimard, 1975. Contains "Apparition
de Larry" and a photograph of Durrell.

Foster, M. A. *THE WARRIORS OF DAWN*. New York:
DAW Books, 1975. Paperback. Contains
'Han signalled the keeper to wait to
awaken her until the dream was over.
Presently she shifted position. An idle
thought flashed through his mind, a
remark of the classical writer, Durrell--
"unfair to watch a sleeping woman."'

LINGUISTICS IN LITERATURE, I: 1 (1975). Contains
Joan Mellard, "The Unity of Lawrence
Durrell's *Alexandria Quartet* (1)."

Lowengard, Manfred. *HOW TO ANALYZE YOUR HAND-
WRITING*. London: Marshall Cavendish,
1975. Contains a photograph of Durrell,
a sample of his handwriting, and a short

analysis: 'There is, . . a syllable-
impulse rather than a word-impulse,
pointing to a man who thinks before he
acts.'

NOTES ON CONTEMPORARY LITERATURE, V: 3 (1975).
Contains George Y. Trail, "Durrell's Io:
A Note on *Tunc* and *Nunquam*."

Pelletier, Jacques. *LE QUATUOR D'ALEXANDRIE DE
LAWRENCE DURRELL*. Paris: Hachette, 1975.

Sajavaara, Karl. *IMAGERY IN LAWRENCE DURRELL'S
PROSE*. Helsinki: Societé Eneophilologique,
1975.

Vinson, J., ed. *CONTEMPORARY POETS*. London:
St. Martin's Press, 1975. Contains an
entry on Durrell composed of biography,
bibliography, a comment by Durrell on
the diversity of his work, and an article
by G. S. Fraser.

———. *CONTEMPORARY NOVELISTS*. London: St.
Martin's Press, 1975. Contains an entry
on Durrell composed of biography,
bibliography, and an article by Alan
Warren Friedman.

THE BOOK COLLECTOR (London), XXIV: 2 (Summer
1975). Contains James A. Brigham, "Note
384: Lawrence Durrell and the *International
Post*."

JOURNAL OF THE HELLENIC DIASPORA, III (July
1975). Contains Thomas Doulis, "Stratis
Tsirkas, The Voice from the Cellar,"
which also discusses *The Alexandria
Quartet*.

WRITER'S DIGEST, LV (November 1975). Contains
Merleen O'Connor Lis, "The *Writer's*

Digest Interview: Lawrence Durrell."

THE RADIO TIMES (London), CCX: 2,731 (13-19
March 1976). Contains John Heilpern,
"Portrait of the Artist as Expatriate."
With a colour portrait of Durrell seated
in his home in Provence.

THE DAILY TELEGRAPH (London) (15 March 1976).
Contains Sylvia Clayton, "Durrell: Gifted
Guide to Greek Islands."

WESTERN HUMANITIES REVIEW, XXX: 2 (Spring 1976).
Contains Steven G. Kellman, "The Self-
Begetting Novel."

Bradbury, Malcolm. *WHO DO YOU THINK YOU ARE?*
London: Secker & Warburg, 1976. Contains
"Voluptia," a parody of the style of *The
Alexandria Quartet*, written by Bradbury
and Michael Orsler. ["Voluptia" first
appeared in *The Guardian*.]

*FAUST BLATTER: HALBJAHRESSCHRIFT DER FAUST-
GESELLSCHAFT*, XXXI (1976). Contains
Hans-Peter M. Gerhardt, "Durrells *An
Irish Faustus* als Beispiel einer modernen
angelsachsischen Auspragung der
Faustfigur."

Friedman, Alan Warren, ed. *FORMS OF MODERN
BRITISH FICTION*. Austin: University of
Texas Press, 1976. Contains John
Unterecker, "Fiction at the Edge of
Poetry: Durrell, Beckett, Green."

Hoops, Wiklef. *DIE ANTINOMIE VON THEORIE UND
PRAXIS IN LAWRENCE DURRELLS ALEXANDRIA
QUARTET: EINE STRUKTURUNTERSUCHUNG.
Europaische Hochschulschriften: Reihe 14,
Angelsachsische Sprache und Literatur,
Bd. 43.* Frankfurt: Peter Lang; Bern:

Herbert Lang, 1976.

Jennings, Elizabeth. *SEVEN MEN OF VISION: AN APPRECIATION*. London: Vision Press, 1976. Contains "Lawrence Durrell: The Vision of the Observer."

---. New York: Barnes and Noble, 1976.

MODERN BRITISH LITERATURE, I: 1 (1976). Contains James Van Dyck Card, "'Tell Me, Tell Me': The Writer as Spellbinder in Lawrence Durrell's *Alexandria Quartet*."

MODERN LANGUAGE STUDIES, VI: 1 (1976). Contains John M. Lennon, "Pursewarden's Death: 'A Stray Brick from Another Region.'"

Nin, Anaïs *THE DIARY OF ANAIS NIN, 1955-1966*. Edited and with a Preface by Gunther Stuhlmann. New York: Harcourt, Brace Jovanovich, 1976. Contains references to Durrell and photographs of Durrell and his family taken during Nin's visit in 1958.

Patrides, C. A., ed. *ASPECTS OF TIME*. Manchester: Manchester University Press, 1976. Contains Ambrose Gordon, "Time, Space, and Eros: *The Alexandria Quartet* Rehearsed," reprinted from *Six Contemporary Novels* (1962).

REVISTA DE ISTORIE SI THEORIE LITERARA, XXV: 3 (1976). Contains Catrinel Plesu Petrulian, "Lawrence Durrell's Quartet."

Stade, George, ed. *SIX CONTEMPORARY BRITISH NOVELISTS*. New York: Columbia University Press, 1976. Contains John Unterecker, "Lawrence Durrell," an updated version of his pamphlet in the *Columbia Essays* on *Modern Writers* series (1964).

---.   New York: Columbia University Press,
1980.

DESCANT (Toronto), XIV (Summer 1976). Contains
Robert McDonald, "Lawrence Durrell:
Classical Puppeteer," an interview on
22 November 1975 in London, 'originally
recorded for the CBC radio program
"Sunday Supplement."'

NOTES AND QUERIES (Oxford), n.s. XXIII: 7
(July 1976). Contains James A. Brigham,
"Addenda to the Bibliography of Lawrence
Durrell."

ROCKY MOUNTAIN REVIEW OF LANGUAGE AND LITERATURE,
XXX: 1 (Winter 1976). Contains Willis
E. McNelly, "Lawrence Durrell's 'Science
Fiction in the True Sense.'"

SMALL PRESS REVIEW, VIII (December 1976).
Contains Merritt and Robin Michelle
Clifton, "The Watch: Small Press
Chronology XV, Supplement--Small Press
Records of Selected Major Authors."

FRANKFURTER ALLGEMEINE ZEITUNG (Frankfurt)
(29 Marz 1977). Contains Günter Blöcker,
"Wo Ehrfurcht ist, strahlt sogar ein
Hundezahn Licht aus. Lawrence Durrells
Roman *Monsieur, oder Der Fürst der
Finsternis.*"

DIE WELT (Hamburg) (23 April 1977). Contains
Otto F. Beer, "Monsieur Satan regiert
die Welt. In Lawrence Durrells neuem
Roman ist die Kraft des 'Guten Gottes'
gebrochen."

THE TIMES LITERARY SUPPLEMENT (London), No. 3,931

(15 July 1977). Contains Alfred
Alexander, "Circular Tour," a review of
Sicilian Carousel.

THE AUTHOR SPEAKS: SELECTED PW INTERVIEWS
1967-1976. New York: Bowker, 1977.
Contains an article on Durrell by Barbara
A. Bannon which first appeared in
Publisher's Weekly for 22 April 1968.

Creed, Walter G. *THE MUSE OF SCIENCE AND THE*
ALEXANDRIA QUARTET. Norwood, Pa.: Norwood
Editions, 1977.

---. Folcroft, Pa.: Folcroft Library Editions,
1978.

Fraser, G. S. *ESSAYS ON TWENTIETH-CENTURY POETS.*
Leicester: Leicester University Press,
1977. Paperback. Contains "Lawrence
Durrell."

Girodias, Maurice. *J'ARRIVE!: UNE JOURNEE SUR*
LA TERRE. Paris: Stock, 1977. Contains
a section on Nancy and Lawrence Durrell's
stay in Paris and the publishing of *The*
Black Book.

Pinchin, Jane Lagoudis. *ALEXANDRIA STILL:*
FORSTER, DURRELL AND CAVAFY. Princeton
Essays in Literature. Princeton, N.J.:
Princeton University Press, 1977.
[Library of Congress Cataloguing in
Publication data identifies Durrell as
"Durrell, Lawrence Wood, 1888-." This
mistake subsequently shows up in countless
bibliographies, indexes and library
catalogues. L. W. Durrell is a botanist:
the confusion may stem from L. G.
Durrell's publication of *The Plant-Magic*
Man (1973).]

THE DAILY TELEGRAPH (London) (4 August 1977).
Contains Selina Hastings, "Durrell on a
Package," a review of *Sicilian Carousel*.

TIME (New York) (29 August 1977). Contains
Lance Morrow, "Bus Stops," a review of
Sicilian Carousel. Illustrated.

SATURDAY REVIEW, IV: 23 (3 September 1977).
Contains Paul Fussell, "Durrell
Incognito," an extended review of
Sicilian Carousel.

NEW YORK TIMES BOOK REVIEW (4 September 1977).
Contains Joan Rodman Goulianos, "Guided
Tour," a review of *Sicilian Carousel*.

DEUS LOCI: THE LAWRENCE DURRELL NEWSLETTER
(Kelowna, B.C.), I: 1 (September 1977).
Edited by James A. Brigham and Ian S.
MacNiven. Contains Theodore Stephanides,
"First Meeting with Lawrence Durrell, and
The House at Kalami;" F.-J. Temple,
"Durrell and France;" James A. Brigham,
"Epigram for an Old Bun-Nosed Tibetan,"
and J. W. G. Dudley, "Bibliography."

ENCOUNTER, XLIX (September 1977). Contains Jan
Morris, "Durrell--on a Tourist Bus?" An
extended review of *Sicilian Carousel*.

CHRISTIAN SCIENCE MONITOR (2 November 1977).
Contains Roderick Nordell, "Durrell in
Sicily: Rich Prose from a Bus," a review
of *Sicilian Carousel*.

DEUS LOCI: THE LAWRENCE DURRELL NEWSLETTER
(Kelowna, B.C.), I: 2-3 (March 1978).
Contains Alan G. Thomas, "Durrell at Parke
Bernet," and Pierre-Marie Michel, "Down
the Styx."

DER ABEND (Berlin) (8 Marz 1978). Contains
CIS, "Teufel im Leib. Lawrence Durrell:
Monsieur, oder der Fürst der Finsternis."

LES NOUVELLES LITTERAIRES, No. 2629 (30 Mars
1978). Contains Jean-Louis Ezine,
"Lawrence Durrell: Villageois Français."

NEW STATESMAN, XCV: 2465 (14 April 1978).
Contains Julian Barnes, "Wordpower," a
review of (among others) "Spirit of Place:
Lawrence Durrell's Egypt" on BBC2, 9 April
1978.

THE LISTENER (London), XCIX (20 April 1978).
Contains "Alexandria and After," an
interview between Lawrence Durrell and
Peter Adam from "Spirit of Place: Lawrence
Durrell's Egypt."

DEUS LOCI: THE LAWRENCE DURRELL NEWSLETTER
(Kelowna, B.C.), I: 4 (June 1978).
Contains Lawrence Thornton, "Narcissism
and Selflessness in *The Alexandria
Quartet*;" "Bibliography."

Amoruso, Vito, and Francesco Binni, eds. *I
CONTEMPORANEI: LETTERATURA INGLESE.* Rome:
Luciano Lucarini, 1978. Contains Giuseppe
Sertoli, "Lawrence Durrell."

ANGLISTICA (Italy), XXI (1978). Contains Anna
Maria Bernini Santere, "Cultura e Tempe
nella piu Recente Narrative Durrelliana."

Brassaï. *HENRY MILLER: ROCHER HEREUX.* Paris:
Gallimard, 1978. Contains a photograph
of and numerous references to Durrell.

Durrell, Gerald. *THE GARDEN OF THE GODS.*
London: Collins, 1978. [Another volume of
reminiscences of the Durrells on Corfu.]

---. *Fauna and Family*. New York: Simon &
    Schuster, 1979.

DER GROSSE BROCKHAUS IN 12 BAENDEN, III.
    Wiesbaden: Brockhaus, 1978. Contains
    "Lawrence Durrell."

Hordequin, Paul. *LES VINGT-TROIS SIECLES DE
    LAWRENCE DURRELL*. France: Henri Veyrier,
    1978.

STUDI INGLESE, 5 (Italy 1978). Contains
    Adriana Musumarra, "Mite e Metafera
    nell'Alessandria di Lawrence Durrell."

DEUS LOCI: THE LAWRENCE DURRELL NEWSLETTER
    (Kelowna, B.C.), II: 1 (September 1978).
    Contains James P. Carley, "Lawrence
    Durrell and the Gnostics," and Leslie W.
    Jones, "'Selected Fictions': The
    Intersection of Life and Art in *The
    Alexandria Quartet*."

THE TIMES (London) (26 October 1978). Contains
    "London Diary," a column on Durrell's
    reasons for taking up 'the flaccid cause
    of Basic English.'

INTERNATIONAL HERALD TRIBUNE, No. 29,788
    (17 November 1978). Contains an
    interview with Durrell by Galina Vromen.
    [Viking Press reprinted a slightly
    abridged version of this interview as an
    insert for review copies of *Livia*.]

DEUS LOCI: THE LAWRENCE DURRELL NEWSLETTER
    (Kelowna, B.C.), II: 2 (December 1978).
    Contains Barbara Anderson, "The Cinematic
    Qualities of Lawrence Durrell's *Alexandria
    Quartet*."

MOSAIC (Winnipeg, Man.), XI: 2 (Winter 1978).

Contains Ian S. MacNiven, "A Room in the
House of Art: The Friendship of Anaïs Nin
and Lawrence Durrell."

DEUS LOCI: THE LAWRENCE DURRELL NEWSLETTER
(Kelowna, B.C.), II: 3 (March 1979).
Contains James A. Brigham, "An
Unacknowledged Trilogy," and Frederick
Goldberg, *The Dark Labyrinth*: Journeys
Beneath the Landscape."

MALAHAT REVIEW (Victoria, B.C.), No. 49 (1979).
Contains Roger Bowen, "Native and Exile:
The Poetry of Bernard Spencer," which
mentions Durrell frequently.

DEUS LOCI: THE LAWRENCE DURRELL NEWSLETTER
(Kelowna, B.C.), II: 4 (June 1979).
Contains Jennifer Linton Fruin, "The
Importance of Narouz in Durrell's Hermetic
Paradigm," and Carol Marshall Peirce,
"'Wrinkled Deep in Time': *The Alexandria
Quartet* as Many-Layered Palimpsest."

Cornu, Marie Renée. *LA DYNAMIQUE DU QUATUOR
D'ALEXANDRIE DE LAWRENCE DURRELL: TROIS
ETUDES.* Montreal: Didier, 1979.

Drescher, Horst W., ed. *LEXIKON DER ENGLISCHEN
LITERATUR.* Stuttgart: Kröner, 1979.
Contains the entries "Lawrence Durrell"
and *"Alexandria Quartet,"* both by Karl
Heinz Stoll.

Durrell, Gerald. *THE PICNIC AND SUCHLIKE
PANDEMONIUM.* London: Collins, 1979.
[Another volume in Gerald Durrell's family
adventures.]

---. *The Picnic and Other Inimitable Stories.*
New York: Simon & Schuster, 1980.

Festa-McCormick, Diana. *THE CITY AS CATALYST:
A STUDY OF TEN NOVELS*. Rutherford, N.Y.:
Fairleigh Dickinson University, 1979.
Contains "Durrell's *Alexandria Quartet*:
'A Whore among Cities'."

Miller, Henry. *BOOK OF FRIENDS, III: JOEY--A
LOVING PORTRAIT OF ALFRED PERLES TOGETHER
WITH SOME BIZARRE EPISODES RELATING TO
THE OTHER SEX*. Santa Barbara, Cal.:
Capra Press, 1979. Durrell appears in
the opening section: 'Though in his later
writings Durrell became a hermetic writer,
in character and behavior at this point in
his career, he was a jolly lusty Dada-
Surrealist son-of-a-bitch like Joey and
myself.'

NUEVA ESTAFETA, XI (1979). Contains Cesar
Antonio Molina, "Un Tiovivo Varado."

Scholes, Robert. *FABULATION AND METAFICTION*.
Champaign: University of Illinois Press,
1979. [Essentially an expansion of his
The Fabulators (1967).]

SURVEY OF SCIENCE FICTION. Englewood Cliffs,
N.J.: Salem Press, 1979. Contains a
discussion of *Tunc* and *Nunquam* by Willis
E. McNelly.

LABRYS (London), 5: *LAWRENCE DURRELL* (1979).
Edited by John Matthews and Grahaeme
Barrasford Young. Contains personal
reminiscences by Jean Fanchette, David
Gascoyne, Gerald Durrell, Freya Stark,
Henry Miller, George Seferis and Diana
Menuhin, and commentaries by Seferis,
Alain Bosquet, Peter Levi, Derek Stanford,
Ken Richardson, J. R. Morrison, Tone
Rugset, James A. Brigham, and Tambimuttu.
[Ordinary edition paperbound. Signed

copies, paperbound, limited to 30 copies.
Signed, clothbound edition limited to 12
copies. Special binding with silver
inset, limited to 8 copies (one for
Durrell, two for publishers, five for
sale; signed).]

THE MALAHAT REVIEW (Victoria, B.C.), No. 51
(July 1979). Contains James P. Carley,
"An Interview with Lawrence Durrell on the
Background to *Monsieur* and Its Sequels."

DEUS LOCI: THE LAWRENCE DURRELL NEWSLETTER
(Kelowna, B.C.), III: 1 (September 1979).
Contains Alan G. Thomas and James A.
Brigham, "One Hundred and Three Addenda;"
"Work in Progress."

---. III: 2 (December 1979). Contains Carol
Marshall Peirce, "A Reading of Durrell's
Map: John Wain's Oxford Lecture," and
James R. Nichols, "Lawrence Durrell's
Alexandria Quartet: The Paradise of Bitter
Fruit."

*BRITISH WRITERS ABROAD: THE MIDLAND BANK GROUP
CALENDAR FOR 1980* (London). Contains a
note, two small portraits, facsimile
signatures, and an extract from *Spirit of
Place*. [The picture for May, upon which
page Durrell appears, is of the Ramesseum,
Thebes, Egypt.]

DEUS LOCI: THE LAWRENCE DURRELL NEWSLETTER
(Kelowna, B.C.), III: 3 (March 1980).
Contains Theodore Stephanides, "In Egypt
after the Fall of Crete," and Grover Koger,
"Some Contributions to the Lawrence
Durrell Bibliography."

INTERNATIONAL HERALD TRIBUNE (11 June 1980).
Contains Irving Marder, "The Topic of

Miller," an obituary article with the remark 'Durrell remains his greatest disciple.'

PARIS MATCH, No. 1621 (20 Juin 1980). Contains Jean Noli, "Henry Miller: l'Ecrivain Maudit Qui A Vaincu Sa Malediction." Portraits, including one of Durrell sliding into Miller's hospital bed in California.

DEUS LOCI: THE LAWRENCE DURRELL NEWSLETTER (Kelowna, B.C.), III: 4 (June 1980). Contains Michael Cartwright, "Playwright as Miracle-Worker: *An Irish Faustus*," and Jennifer Waelti-Walters, "Coincidental Perceptions (Michel Butor and Lawrence Durrell)."

Fussell, Paul. *ABROAD: BRITISH LITERARY TRAVELLING BETWEEN THE WARS*. Oxford: Oxford University Press, 1981. Contains some references to Durrell's stay in Corfu.

Girodias, Maurice. *THE FROG PRINCE*. New York: Crown, 1980. Girodias' father, Jack Kahane, was the first publisher of *The Black Book*. Durrell appears in this autobiography.

Kellman, Steven G. *THE SELF-BEGETTING NOVEL*. New York: Columbia University Press, 1980. Contains "One Quartet and Four Notebooks," the latter a reference to Doris Lessing's *Golden Notebook*.

Krementz, Jill. *THE WRITER'S IMAGE: THE LITERARY PORTRAITS OF JILL KREMENTZ*. With a Preface by Kurt Vonnegut and an Introduction by Trudy Butner Krisher. Boston: David R. Godine, 1980. Contains the frequently reproduced photograph of Durrell visiting Miller while the latter recovered from surgery.

Nin, Anaïs. *THE DIARY OF ANAIS NIN, 1966-1974.* Edited and with a Preface by Gunther Stuhlmann. New York: Harcourt, Brace Jovanovich, 1980.

PER LAWRENCE DURRELL. Brescia, Italy: Shakespeare & Company, 1980. With a Preface by Giuseppe Sertoli. Contains articles by Miller, Perlès, Temple, Aldington and Steiner, all previously published but translated into Italian for the first time, and an article by Alberto Boatto which had not previously appeared anywhere.

RETURN TO OASIS: WAR POEMS AND RECOLLECTIONS FROM THE MIDDLE EAST, 1940-1946. See Section C.32.

PARIS MATCH, No. 1,623 (4 Juillet 1980). Contains Maurice Girodias, "Miller, Mon Ami," an obituary article, with references to Durrell.

MACLEAN'S (Toronto), XCIII: 35 (1 September 1980). Contains Mark Abley, "Gerald Durrell: A Passionate Zoo Keeper and Other Animals." With a reference to Larry Durrell.

THE SUNDAY TIMES MAGAZINE (14 September 1980). Contains Andrew Sanger, "A Life in the Day of Lawrence Durrell." Interview, with a color photograph by Harold Chapman.

THE EVENING NEWS (London) (25 September 1980). Contains Lee Wilson, "The Guru of Tender Sex Knows how to Live For Ever," comments on *A Smile in the Mind's Eye* and *Collected Poems 1931-1974* (both published 1980).

THE LISTENER (London) (25 September 1980). Contains Mary Warnock, "Chang's Visit," a review of *A Smile in the Mind's Eye.* Portrait.

THE GUARDIAN (Manchester) (26 September 1980). Contains Andrew Sanger, "The Poetic Devil in the Holy Water; after the *Quartet*, the Quincunx, and at last, the *Collected Poems.*" Portrait.

DEUS LOCI: THE LAWRENCE DURRELL NEWSLETTER (Kelowna, B.C.), IV: 1 (September 1980). Contains Reed Way Dasenbrock, "Death and the Counterlife of Heresy in Wyndham Lewis and Lawrence Durrell."

LABRYS (London), 6 (September 1980). Contains a review by John Matthews of *Collected Poems 1931-1974* and *A Smile in the Mind's Eye.*

THE SUNDAY OBSERVER (London) (5 October 1980). Contains "Last of the Romantics," a 'Pendennis' column which makes a point of being not very politely rude.

THE DAILY TELEGRAPH (London) (16 October 1980). Contains a review by Major-General Edward Fursdon of *Return to Oasis* (see Section C.32).

THE NEW STATESMAN AND NATION (London) (31 October 1980). Contains David Sweetman, "Princely Pyknic," a review of *A Smile in the Mind's Eye* and *Collected Poems 1931-1974.*

THE OBSERVER (London) (9 November 1980). Contains Gavin Ewart, "Sunlight and

Surrealism," a review of *Collected Poems 1931-1974*.

THE VANCOUVER SUN (Vancouver, B.C.) (29 November 1980). Contains Bill Davies, "Durrell's Greek Islands: From Vampires to Tourists," one of the "Armchair Traveller" series. Illustrated with a photograph of the cover of *The Greek Islands*.

DEUS LOCI: THE LAWRENCE DURRELL NEWSLETTER (Kelowna, B.C.), IV: 2 (December 1980). Contains Patrick von Richtofen, "Lawrence Durrell, Prince of Denmark."

FRANKFURTER ALLGEMEINE ZEITUNG (Frankfurt) (2 Januar 1981). Contains Gerhard Kirchner, "Kutsche ins Freudenhaus. Lawrence Durrells Roman *Livia*."

THE SUNDAY OBSERVER (London) (15 February 1981). Contains Robert Chesshyre, "Bitter Fruit across the Peace Line," an "Away" column about Cyprus which contains several references to Durrell and to his house in Bellapaix.

DEUS LOCI: THE LAWRENCE DURRELL NEWSLETTER (Kelowna, B.C.), IV: 3 (March 1981). Contains Kent Ekberg, "Studio 28: The Influence of the Surrealist Cinema on the Early Fiction of Anaïs Nin and Henry Miller."

---. IV: 4 (June 1981). Contains George Cleyet, "The Villa Seurat Circle: Creative Nexus," and Ian S. MacNiven, "A Map of Durrell's Inner World?"

ILLUSTRATIONS

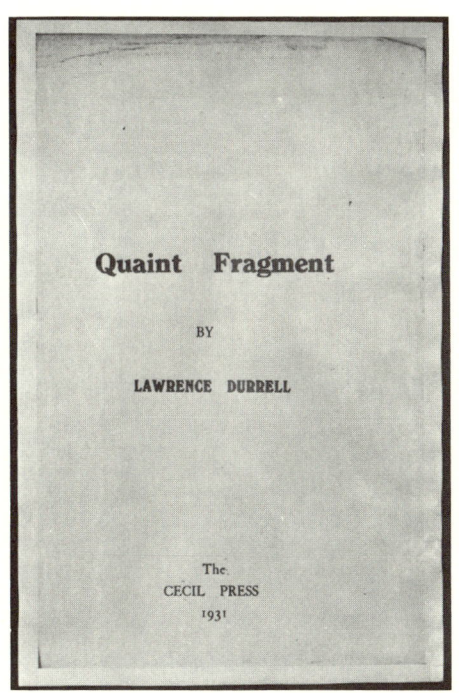

Quaint Fragment

BY

LAWRENCE DURRELL

The
CECIL PRESS
1931

TEN POEMS

BY
LAWRENCE DURRELL

Ballade of Slow Decay

Christmas
1932

BROMO BOMBASTES

By
GAFFER PEESLAKE

CADUCEUS PRESS
16 Grenville Street, London, W.C. 1

179

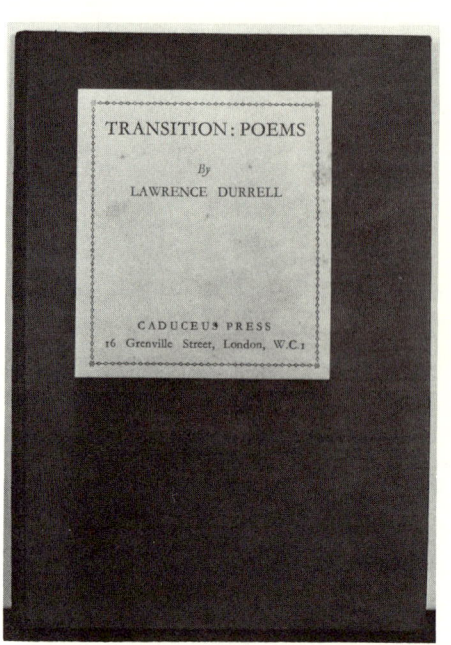

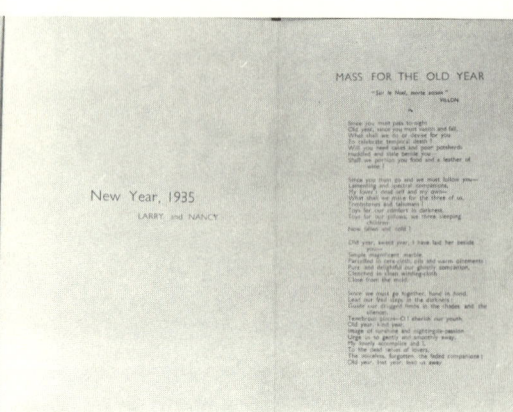

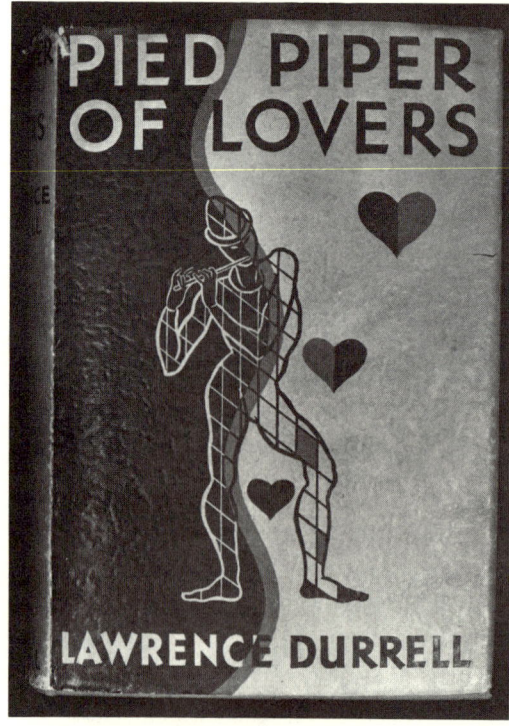

180

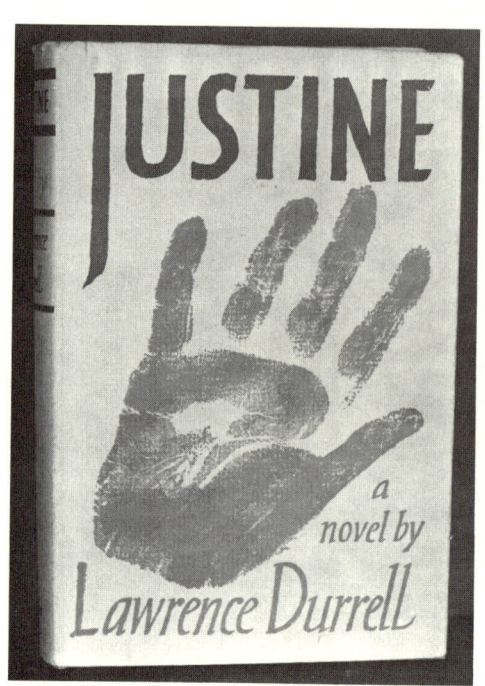

184

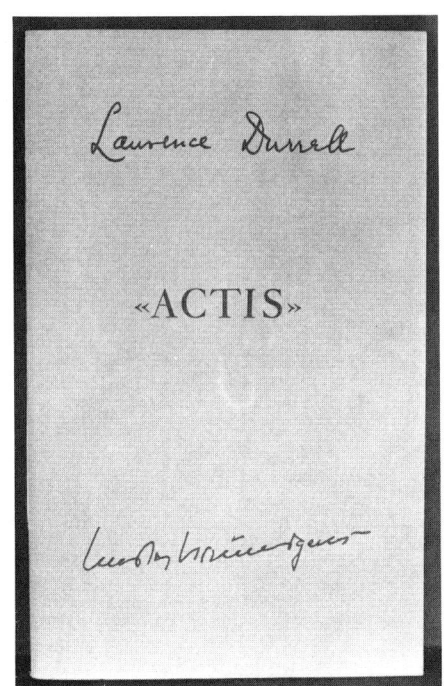

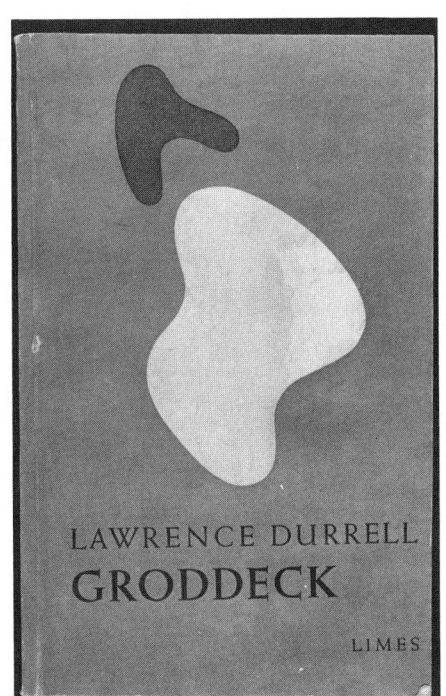

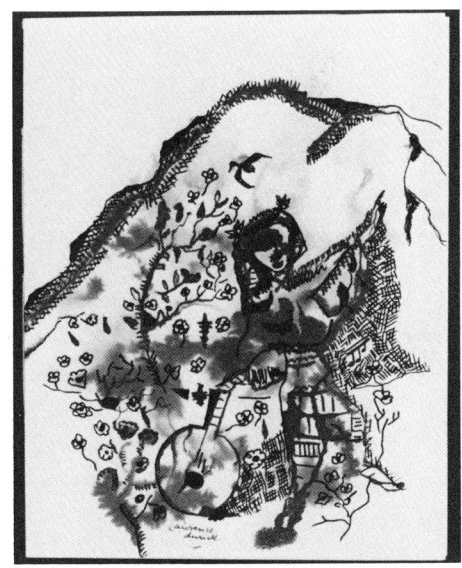

185

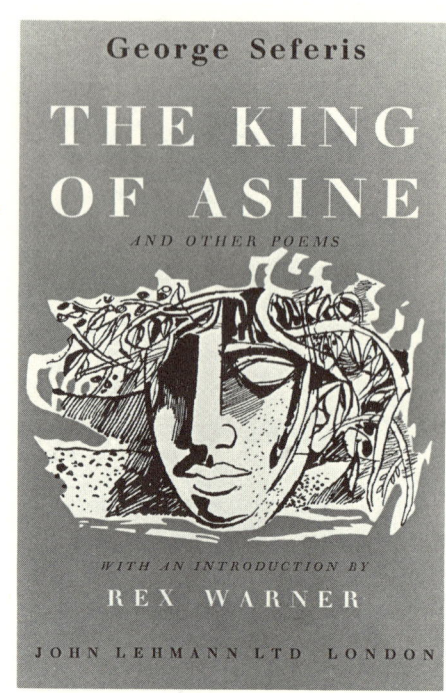

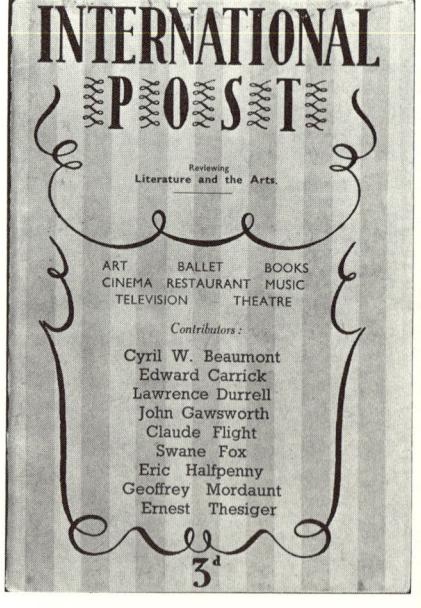

INDEX